ROADMAP TO HIGH GALDR RUNE WORK

By Frank A. Rúnaldrar

HIGH GALDR SERIES
Book One: The Breath of Oðin Awakens (2nd Ed)
Book Two: The Spirit of Húnir Awakens (Part 1)
Book Three: The Spirit of Húnir Awakens (Part 2)
Book Four: The Blood of Lóðurr Awakens
Book Five: Roadmap to High Galdr Rune Work

QUESTIONS & ANSWERS SERIES
The Breath of Oðin Awakens - Questions & Answers
The Spirit of Húnir Awakens - Questions & Answers

ROADMAP TO HIGH GALDR RUNE WORK

A Consolidated Study Guide

by
Frank A. Rúnaldrar

Part of the High Galdr Series
www.highgaldr.com

Published in 2019 by:
Bastian & West
www.bastianandwest.com

Copyright © 2019 Frank A. Rúnaldrar

The moral right of the author has been asserted.

All rights reserved. No part of this publication may be reproduced or transmitted in any form or by any means, electronic or mechanical, including photocopying, recording, or by any information storage and retrieval system, without permission in writing from the copyright holder. Reviewers may quote brief passages.

Part of High Galdr Series
www.highgaldr.com

ISBN: 978-0-9955343-7-7

A CIP catalogue record for this book is available from the British Library.

Editor: James Millington
In-book illustrator: Ben Hansen

Book typeset in Niva Light by PeGGO Fonts, Norse font by Joël Carrouché and runic elements in Felt-Tip Futhark by Thomas Kaeding

Copyright Notice: All rights, title and interests in the copyrights to all materials (including but not limited to any proprietary knowledge, data, information, manuals, illustrations, diagrams, flowcharts, marks or other information therein contained or thereby disclosed and representing the author's original works), are hereby reserved and to be considered the exclusive property of and belong exclusively to the author. The purchase of this book by any person(s), and its usage by any other party, shall not be construed as granting or conferring any rights by license or otherwise to the purchasing party or any other party who may come in possession of the book and/or its materials. No part of this publication or its materials may be reproduced, distributed, disseminated, or transmitted in any form or by any means and for any purpose, including but not limited to photo-copying, recording, or other electronic or mechanical methods, without the prior written permission and consent of the author, except in the case of brief quotations embodied in critical reviews and certain other non-commercial used permitted by copyright law. In the event any reader or third party submits to the author or the publisher, either jointly or severally, any questions, then any questions based on, derived from or incorporating any of the author's materials in this publication, together with any answers provided by the author, if any, shall be deemed to be works derived from the author's copyrighted materials and accordingly such reader or third party in submitting its questions irrevocably agrees to the exclusive and royalty free world wide transfer and assignment (free of costs) of all or any rights, title or benefit in such questions to the owner for its discretionary use in any format and by any medium.

Usage Disclaimer: It is expressly agreed and acknowledged by all and any reader(s) and any parties that come into possession of the materials that all materials, information, techniques, methods, processes or statements made in this publication, and all and any associated materials as may be derived therefrom and distributed from time to time in any written or tangible forms and in any media (including electronic media), as the case may be, by the author or its publisher(s), are for to be used strictly for educational purposes only (the "Permitted Purpose") and not for any other personal or commercial purpose. All materials reflect the author's personal views and opinions, and no method or process or statement or anything else said in the materials is to be treated as having any scientific value, validity or status. Under no circumstances whatsoever or howsoever are any materials in this book, in whole or in part, intended to operate as scientifically proven methods, processes or statements, or intended to offer any medical or other advise, or be used in substitute for medical advise of and/or treatment by physicians for any matters. Neither the author nor its publisher(s) make any statement, representation, guarantee or undertaking howsoever or whatsoever as to the usefulness of any materials. The use of the materials for any other purpose, including any personal or commercial purposes other than for educational purposes, contrary to the Permitted Purpose, is not promoted and strictly prohibited. The author and its publisher(s) accept no risk, responsibility or liability for any unsanctioned use, which shall be at the user's sole risk, and shall, together and severally (the "Released and Indemnified Parties"), be held harmless and indemnified by any users engaging in any unsanctioned use contrary to this disclaimer from all and any claims, rights, liabilities, demands, obligations, conditions, promises, acts, costs, expenses, accountings, damages or actions of whatsoever kind or nature, whether in law or otherwise, whether known or unknown, which they made have or may thereafter have against the Released and Indemnified Parties for or by any reason of any occurrence, matter or thing which arise or are claimed to have arisen out of or in connection with any such unsanctioned use of the materials.

I would like to dedicate this to everyone studying the Runes...

Table of Content

Roadmap To High Galdr Rune Work
- Definitions of Norse Terms I
- Introducing... High Galdr Vii
- The Norse Tradition - Heritage of the Indo-Europeans .. xi
  - The Eddas xi
  - The Saga(s) xiv

Essential Practices From The Breath of Oðin Awakens
- Key Work from the Breath of Oðin Awakens 1
- Understanding the Hamingja, Megin and Önd 3
- Awakening the Hamingja 9
- Awakening the Core of the Self 17
- Awakening the Breath of Oðin 25

Essential Practices From The Spirit of Húnir Awakens
- Key Work from the Spirit of Húnir Awakens 39
- Understanding the Óðr, Hugr and Minni 43
- Deeper Insights into Actual Óðr 45
- The Hugr and Minni: Functional Manifestations of the Óðr 49
- Mind, Spirit or Spirit-Mind Unveiling the Hugr 53
- Becoming Conscious of the Óðr (Spirit) 55
- Spirit and Senses - Awakening and Development . 61
  - Using Óðr Directly from Within the Physical 63
- Awakening Higher Levels of Sensory Perception . 65
- The Óðr and Shaping the Spirit 71
- Óðr Shaping Into Runes - Becoming the Rune Flow . 75
- Communication and Use of the Hugr Raven 79
- Setting the Hugr Raven to Flight 81

Essential Pracitces from The Blood of Lóðurr Awakens

- Key Work from the Blood of Lóðurr Awakens 91
- Body Awareness - Biological Awareness 93
- Functions of Biological Awareness 97
- Awakening the Bodily Awareness & Intelligence.101
- Body Shapes and Energy Types 109
  - Body Types 109
  - Body Shapes as Energy Indicators 111
- Impact of Body Form
  - The Three Fundamental Forces 115
    - A Few Words on Muscle 120
    - A Few Words on the Nervous System 122
  - Energy Body (Hamr) Fundamentals 125
    - The Cycle of Existence of the Hamr 127
  - Perceiving the Energy Body (Hamr) 129
  - Seeing the Energy of the Energy Body (Hamr) Sphere..135
  - Connecting with the Energy Body (Hamr) 137
    - Establishing the Connection 139
    - Gender Advantages 140

Intent

- The Great Mystery of Intent 145
  - What Exactly Is Intent 145
  - Limitations Imposed Upon Intent 146
- Mastering Intent – Part I: Pure Thought 149
- Mastering Intent – Part II: Biological Sensing 153
- Mastering Intent – Part III: Streaming of Intent..157
  - Pulling the Self into the Lik 159

Visualisation

- The Art of Visualisation 165
  - Positioning Visualisations 168
  - Visualisation Vs Imagination 171

Appendixes

- Appendix A: Table of Runic Names in Icelandic & Germanic 179

- Appendix B: References & Footnotes 183

Forthcoming Titles 185

Table of Illustrations

Hamingja location on upper-back 5, 11
Personified Hamingja formed behind the
   physical body (Lik) 20
DNA charged & empowered megin flow 27
Spirit (Óðr) inside the energy body (Hamr)
   inside the physical body (Lik) 56
Hugr Raven rising out of left side of the brain ... 83
Female body shapes 112
Male body shapes 113
Flowing force body shapes 117
Solidifying force body shapes 118
Burning force body shapes 119
Trance & meditation (sitting) position 129
Spherically shaped energy body 130
Egg shaped energy body 131
Visualisation range 170

Notes from the Publisher

Following the release of *The Blood of Lóðurr Awakens*, we decided to release this additional title in the High Galdr series to provide for those who have not had the opportunity to work through all the previous titles to cover the essential key skills. *Roadmap to High Galdr Rune Work - A Consolidated Study Guide* provides you with a cut-down curriculum designed to offer the key practices you will need to master in preparation for High Galdr itself. Working through this title will give you all the essential skills needed to tackle actual Galdr. It will, however, not provide the depth of mastery of the Self which the full volumes do. All we are aiming for in these pages is to cover the absolute minimum needed for High Galdr, whereas the full titles (*The Breath of Oðin Awakens*, *The Spirit of Húnir Awakens - Parts 1 & 2* and *The Blood of Lóðurr Awakens*) do that in addition to developing the corresponding parts of your Self and enabling their eventual mastery for more advanced work. It is important to keep these distinctions in mind when reading through this title.

There is however no reason why you could not work through this title then proceed to learning and practising High Galdr and subsequently tackle the mastery of the Self. This would indeed present a slight shortcut in the entire process since you would be approaching the Self mastery elements with the ability to not only vocalise runes but to actually unleash their full power via High Galdr. Ultimately, how each of us makes headway in this work will depend on the individual. By releasing this 'quick' study title, we are giving you the option to choose your own pace and order of doing things.

A final note is due before moving onto the subject matter. The theory and intellectual analysis of these topics have been kept to an absolute minimum, so if you would like to gain an in-depth understanding of those topics, please refer to the respective titles. Here, you will find the focus to be on the practical side of things, rather than the theoretical. Yes, some loss is incurred by skipping over the theory but that is the purpose of the main titles, not this quick study guide.

Definitions of Norse Terms

All terms used refer to their original Old Norse or Proto-Germanic meanings not their modern day derivatives in the Scandinavian, German or Icelandic languages.

Önd – Part of the psycho-spiritual construct of the Self as viewed in Norse mysticism and mythology, the Önd sits at the apex of the spiritual level of the Self and can be loosely described as 'The Breath of Oðin' or luck / Megin-fulled breath.

Óðr (or Óðr, or Óð) – Part of the psycho-spiritual Self- sitting at the apex of the mental part of the Self, it can be loosely thought of as the conscious awareness or totality of the spirit.

Hugr – The Hugr is often thought of as the reasoning or logic part of the mind, sometimes as the mind itself and often as the intellect or intellectual capacity of the mind. Essentially it is the manifestation of the active characteristics of the Spirit (Óðr).

Minni – The polar opposite of the Hugr and often thought of as the root of memory, the Minni is actually the individual record of one's experiences and acts as an anchor point for those events.

Hamr – The Hamr is the energy body, often described as the blueprint of the physical.

Lik – Part of the psycho-spiritual Self sitting at the apex of the energetic part of the Self, the Lik is the complete physical body as a result of the fusion of matter and spirit via the medium of energy. When talking about the Lik we include everything which is part of it, including the energetic and spiritual elements as well as the typically physical ones such as blood, DNA, nervous system and so forth.

Sal – Part of the psycho-spiritual self sitting at the bottom of the energetic part of the Self, the Sal is often loosely translated as the 'shadow'. In effect, it is the complimentary opposite of the Hamr.

Heimdall – One of the principle Gods in Norse mythology, Heimdall was described as the white god or whitest of the gods. He is linked to light and the pure power thereof. He possesses the resounding horn Gjallarhorn, which he will sound at the time of Ragnarök. He is the God responsible for originating the various classes of mankind and imbuing these with increasing degrees of divinity.

The Æsir – This refers to the clan of Gods from Ásgarð, typically associated with the divine aspects of spiritual origin. They are wielders of the Galdr sciences (use of runes and their correct applications) and have strong connections with the spiritual, awareness, intellect, mind, knowledge and the sciences.

The Vanir – The Vanir refers to the clan of Gods from Vanaheim, typically associated with the natural order of things and having strong connections with nature, the world and the physical as it moves towards the spiritual. They are wielders of Seidr crafts (sorcery, divination, soothsaying, shamanistic practices, herbal medicines and so forth).

Yggdrasil (Mjötvið) – The mythical Ash tree that is home to the nine worlds in Norse cosmology. It is also thought of as being the foundation of the cosmos itself and everything within it.

Egil's Saga – Otherwise termed in Iceland as the Egla, this is an Icelandic Saga dating back to 1240 AD, which details the life of Egil Skallagrimsson a farmer, Viking and poet.

Muspelheim – Muspelheim was the first world to be formed out of the great emptiness called Ginnungagap. It is a realm of flame, fires, light and explosive power unreachable by any not native to it.

Húnir (Hœnir) – One of the Æsir Gods, he helped create mankind along with Oðin and Lóðurr. He gave the first man and woman Óðr and hence imbued them with spirit. He is also one of the Gods who survives Ragnarök and gains prophetic powers thereafter.

Njörðr – Vanir god of the Sea, he is the father of Freya and Frey and was one of the hostages exchanged in the Æsir-Vanir war. It is said he will return to head the Vanir after Ragnarök.

Lóðurr (Lóð or Lóðr) – Lóðurr is a mysterious God, whom academics seem unable to accept other than trying (and failing) to identify him with Loki or even Freyr. He gives the first man and woman blood and hence health, in other words flesh or physicality.

Ragnarök – Also known as the Twilight of the Gods, this final battle was foretold in the Völuspá (stanza 41). It describes the ultimate fate of the Gods themselves.

Ætts – Meaning 'clan', it can also refer to related grouping of concepts, individuals or sets of people. It is sometimes referred to as kin-Ætts which would be used in terms of a grouping of related people. For instance, Ætts in terms of individuals would include related individually such as family, whereas kin-Ætts would expand this to a wider set of relations such as an entire clan.

Norns – This typically refers to the Jotun (giantess) sisters Urð, Verðandi and Skuld who weave the threads of fate for men and gods alike. They also draw water from the Well of Urð and collect sands from around it to pour on the Yggdrasil to prevent it from rotting. The word Norn can also refer to the concept of the fate weaver attached to individuals at birth which could be either good or bad, weaving either a fortunate or unfortunate fate for that individual.

Niflheim – One of the Nine Worlds in Norse Cosmology, Niflheim is a world of primordial ice and cold, sometimes also called the mist world.

Fylgja – Part of the archetypal level of the Self, the Fylgja is a spirit which binds to the individual, becoming a part of him or her upon birth. It is always inherited down the ancestral lines and carries experiential essence and memories and powers of the former Self's embodiment. The Fylgja forms into either animal, humanoid or geometric form depending on evolutionary progress of both the individual and itself.

Kin-Fylgja – Similar to the Fylgja, this overarching spirit carries the experiential essences of the entire family line, the sum resulting from the entire ancestral lines up to the current point. It attaches to the eldest male of the family line and communicates primarily through the females of the line.

Hamingja – The Hamingja is part of the archetypal level of the Self. It manifests as an energetic organ in the individual which stores the Megin (power) it produces from various runic and life energies.

Wyrd and Ørlǫg – This refers to fate or rather threads of fate as they flow through creation. Cosmically, Ørlǫg is seen as infinite fibres of energetic substance flowing throughout all existence. From a human perspective, these fibres appear to flow through Creation but also through individuals, Gods and all life forms, setting the path they will follow over the course of their existence. However, when viewed from a Cosmic perspective, all things in Creation flow through the fibres. The Wyrd refers to these threads on a larger scale such as for humanity as a whole, individual races and clans while Ørlǫg refers to how these threads manifest on the individual level. The Wyrd is formed by the Norns and the Ørlǫg is build from the Wyrd based on individual's power, fate and evolutionary needs by the Fylgja.

Óðrerir (Odhrærir, Óðrørir) – This refers to the container or cauldron which holds the sacred mead. Its equivalent is the legend of the 'Holy Grail' in Arthurian mythology and the 'Holy Chalice' in Christian mythology. The Óðrerir may well have been the inspiration for these later myths.

Introducing... High Galdr

The *Roadmap to High Galdr Rune Work* provides you with all the essential key practices which can be used as a curriculum to give you all the fundamentals needed for High Galdr rune work. Its aims are simple: to prepare you for actual rune work by covering the absolute minimum preparatory material. Unlike the individual books *The Breath of Oðin Awakens*, *The Spirit of Húnir Awakens (Parts 1 & 2)* and *The Blood of Lóðurr Awakens*, its goal is not to fully develop the Self and lead you to mastery of your Self (if you are aiming for that, you should really work through each of them sequentially) but rather, if all you want are the basics so that you can get to the point where actual rune work is possible, then this is the perfect guide!

What is Galdr?

The practice of Galdr is fundamental to the Æsir and was 'taught' to humankind by Heimdall when he revealed the runes to humanity. Subsequently, other teachers from the realms of Ásgarð came forth to various gifted individuals, to teach them more advanced applications of runic practices. Oðin himself came to amplify those teachings throughout his travels and interactions with our ancestors, leading to various written sources being made available, the most notable of which is the Hávamál. Long ago, he even undertook teaching Galdr to the Vanir in exchange for knowledge of the arts of Seiðr. Interestingly, this exchange is an excellent illustration of the practical applications of X Gjöf (Gebo) (the principle of a gift requiring a gift) even at that divine level!

So what is Galdr? One can define it as the uttering of runes, runic formulae, runic chants, runic vocalisation and bind-runes accompanied by their tracing/carving.

In Midgard (Earth), and specifically in relation to humans, these arts were used in a severely limited fashion, which essentially reduced Galdr to vocalisation and writing of the runes. It became a meagre chanting, visualising and tracing of the runes (for the sake of brevity, formulae, chants and bind-runes are herein included when mentioning 'runes'). Worse yet, the concept of Galdr itself has been fused with that of Seiðr. This merging was not done through a harmonious blending of the two arts, but rather aspects of the one were muddled into the other. The underlying fundamentals of Galdr gradually shifted from pure mysticism to those of ritualistic application. In the process, it lost the true power of Galdr itself, which wound up as a shadow of its former potential.

Some might argue that elements of Seiðr are needed in Galdr, such as the induction of trance states found within Seiðr as being essential to the effective use of

Galdr. This is both partly correct and incorrect. While it is true that trance mastery is essential to Galdr, it is incorrect to assume that Seiðr is required or was the only means of achieving the trance (or ecstatic) states. Galdr itself is used to induce a trance state, which can at times even surpass those achieved via Seiðr (in terms of practicality, not potential). This stems from the mystical aspects of Galdr and is the reason why it was deemed, in days long past, to be the sacred science of the Gods.

The 'High Galdr' series seeks to bring back the knowledge and the tools to practice the sacred aspects of Galdr. Due to its nature, many will flock to it. Some will seek to master it and others will seek to abuse it. To the former, all that remains to be said is be persistent and practice; even partial success and minor achievements expand the Self, providing phenomenal gains: new perceptions, skills and abilities, as well as pure wisdom, knowledge and most importantly, the ability to influence reality in a very formulistic (scientific) manner. It becomes the equivalent of coding but in this case, we are coding reality itself! Once fully mastered, there will be nothing left that anyone in Midgard can teach. To the latter, those who seek to abuse High Galdr, a warning: even though High Galdr can be misused, it is vital to remain aware that the Gods protect their mysteries and they themselves throw hurdles in the path and practices of those who are seeking to harm their people, their creation and the cosmic order of things for which they are responsible. Not much else needs to be said on that subject, other than to confirm that no matter how hard those who would abuse them try, these sacred mysteries will always evade full mastery.

- Roadmap to High Galdr Rune Work -

In these pages, you will find instructions to take the preparatory/foundational steps. They will assist in uncovering the mysteries of and awaken the parts of the Self, moving them further towards the divine, and will eventually lead you to uttering the Galdr across multiple levels of reality (both subjectively and objectively). This frees the mind of all the baggage that inhibits our heritage from blooming, enabling you to learn the rune and each rune's specific energy patterns, condense them into reality, and finally unleash them. The microcosmic Yggdrasil within our bodies and the macrocosmic Yggdrasil will be brought into a synchronous harmony as the Self unfolds into its divine birthright.

The Norse Tradition - Heritage of The Indo-Europeans

It is impossibly difficult to determine the full extent of or to search out all sources of the Norse tradition. Most pre-date the widespread availability of writing, while others were passed exclusively from one generation to the next orally. The main sources of knowledge left to us in this modern day and age are found in the Eddas and the Sagas.

The Eddas

The term 'Eddas' comes from Old Norse and it is used by modern-day students and academics to refer to two main Icelandic literary works that serve as the basis of our knowledge of Norse mythology, tradition, teachings and history.

There are two primary Eddas, both written during the 13th Century in Iceland. The first set is grouped under the label 'Poetic Eddas', which predate even the Viking Age, and come from an unknown source.

They are divided into two sections; the first is a narration of the creation, destruction and rebirth of the world and provides the mythology of the Norse deities as well. The second is a set of legends relating to Norse heroes, kings and wise men.

The Poetic Eddas were incorporated into the Codex Regius written during the 13th century. Unfortunately, it was not until the mid-1600s that the Codex resurfaced in the hands of Brynjólfur Sveinsson, a bishop to the Church of Iceland in Skálholt. Brynjólfur was also a scholar at heart, hence his fascination with the old myths and legends! It is he who collected and produced this compilation of Old Norse mythology and heroic poems into the Eddas. However, it is widely accepted that he was not their author and so they were not labelled after him. He gifted his findings to King Christian IV of Denmark in manu-script form, thus earning it the name Codex Regus, which was then preserved in the Royal Library until 1971 when a formal return was made to Iceland.

The second Eddas were compiled from traditional oral sources and (theorised to be derived from) an unknown set of Eddas often referred to as the Elder Eddas by Icelandic scholar Snorri Sturluson (dated from the 14th century). He collated these literary works under the label of Prose Eddas. Like the Poetic Eddas, the Prose Eddas also describe in detail the creation, destruction and rebirth of the world, Norse mythology and life. Due to his background and the time period in which Snorri lived, the 'Christianisation' of certain concepts and legends are to be found in this text. Nonetheless, it does provide an invaluable and rich account of the Norse tradition and, just as importantly, how it was recounted over the generations.

Scholars have long held the view that the Poetic Eddas, and therefore the Prose Eddas, came from a much older source. The rediscovery of what is known as the Elder Eddas helped confirm that suspicion. The Elder Eddas are comprised of the Pagan poems and teachings that were later hinted at in Snorri's Prose Eddas.

Many translations from Old Norse can be found and the number thereof seems to increase steadily over time. One key point to keep in mind is that the Eddas are complex literary works detailing the Norse tradition through poetry and prose. Accordingly, when reading various translations, different terms and words are often found to express the same underlying concept or similar words are used to describe totally different ones. Add to this the fact that many Old Norse terms have no equivalents in modern day languages, and it becomes vitally important to read in between the lines, so to speak, referring back to the concept rather than relying strictly on the words themselves. A literal, legalistic reading that has become completely engrained in the modern readers' minds will fail to capture the actual meanings, concepts and knowledge held within the Eddas.

Aside from those mentioned, other so-called Eddas can be found. These are typically adaptations in use by specific groups based on either the Prose or Poetic Eddas. The key point to note, however, is that those are adaptations.

The translations of the Prose and Poetic Eddas that have been used as source materials for this work can be found in both the references and further reading sections. Modern day adaptations and/or derivatives are not used.

The Saga(s)

Unlike the Eddas, the term Saga (story) refers to one of the many stories, poems, legends and so forth. Not all the Sagas made it into the Eddas. Individual Sagas might have not been discovered until a much later, post-Eddas compilation period.

These Sagas are individual tales in prose or poetic form detailing historical events of heroic deeds, tales or important persons (a great many of them Vikings, Pagans or even sometimes Christians), bishops, saints and even legendary heroes. Many of the Sagas include tales of kings, special individuals (such as the Egil Sagas used in this text), and even territorial historic events ranging from the Nordic countries to the British Isles, France and even North America (Canada in particular)[1]. Their main characteristic is that they are a historical statement or tale (that is the literal meaning of the term Saga). This has raised much speculation as the intellectual machinery attempts to digest material that is these days considered to be supernatural or metaphysical.

This range of subject matter is simply due to the fact that these records were, more often than not, kept within individual families, transmitted orally or simply brought from a different territory. Remember, the Old Norse people (Indo-Europeans) existed long before the Viking age and had to survive forced Christianisation, dispersion of territories, hostile natural environments, and so forth. In other words, these Sagas provided additional insights into the traditions, mythology, legends and teachings that were initially transmitted orally and then, once writing became widely available, were from time to time published. Even to this date, however, many of the Sagas have never been published and are kept from public view for a variety of reasons. Some of these reasons are of a very practical nature. In Iceland, for instance, these stories are considered to be part of the national heritage, hence books or manuscripts that are valued as family heirlooms, if known about, would be confiscated by the state on the basis of it being a national treasure. This is somewhat of an over-simplification but is an example of one of the many reasons why a lot of these Sagas never have (and most probably never will) see the light of public accessibility or dissemination. Others might hold deep-seated hereditary knowledge, which, more often than not, requires specific genetic and energetically transmitted capabilities to be of any use. This is the case with the higher mysteries bestowed upon the Jarls by Heimdall.

Fortunately, many Sagas are available for public consumption, and they do provide an exceptional insight into the wisdom and traditions of our ancestors. In this work, the Sagas are used to illustrate and gain further insights into teachings from older sources, be they part of the oral tradition or those in the Eddas[2].

This seeming endless diversity of sources is what makes studying the Old Norse tradition wildly exciting and fascinating beyond expectation, yet also insanely frustrating. Each Saga and Edda can expand our understanding, yet finding the relevant ones can be a most noteworthy challenge, in addition to actually understanding the knowledge therein once it is found! Nevertheless, gaining a reasonably solid foundation into the tradition is key; it is after all part of our heritage and is what empowers us. The appendices will provide more references and recommended reading. Fear not, however — all Eddas and Sagas relevant to the topics and teachings in this book have been included; for without basing such teachings in the actual texts and other sources of heritage they would hold no validity per se. It is of vital importance to work with these Eddas and Sagas as the foundation upon which we build our spiritual heritage.

ESSENTIAL PRACTICES FROM THE BREATH OF ODIN AWAKENS

Key Work From The Breath of Oðin Awakens

The following section presents initial work you should undertake from *The Breath of Oðin Awakens*. Here, we deal with the first of the gifts of the three Gods to Ask and Embla (the first man and woman, our root ancestors), namely Oðin's gift of Önd (breath) and its associated by-products (Megin and the Hamingja). Essentially, your goal here is to familiarise yourself with the Hamingja and start to increase your available Megin (power) on a regular basis. I would recommend a daily routine until you have become familiar with the practices and then switching to a twice-a-week regular boost. The initial loading will ensure you start countering any deficiencies and give you a head start when it comes to working on the next set of practices. The regular work will ensure that whatever reserves you have used up in your work or those which have been automatically used by your growth are immediately topped up in order to ensure as constant and consistent a moving forward in all your skills and work as possible. This avoids the so-called drop back into the daily operation of consciousness so many experience following a burst of progress. Remember, you need to fuel your abilities and growth – just as you fuel your physical body (Lik) with food, so too the same applies to these other parts of your Self.

Following these initial steps, all that is required at this point in time is the awakening of your conscious awareness to the actual Breath of Oðin. The final part of this section will look at that and ensure you are able to consciously unleash its flow. Once you are comfortable doing so, you will have completed all the essential preliminary work found in *The Breath of Oðin Awakens* and can move onto the next step. I would advise a more complete study of this title as some of the additional skills and insights developed within it are extremely valuable, even if they are not technically speaking 'essential'. It is a relatively small title to work through practically and should not present any major difficulty in doing so.

Understanding the Hamingja, Megin and Önd

It is important to cover the definition of these terms before proceeding forward. Without the understanding of what you are actually trying to use or manipulate, it will be most difficult to do any practical work.

Let us start with looking at what exactly 'Megin' is, and most specifically what this term refers to. Megin causes a lot of confusion in those who are new to this concept (and even to those who are studying/familiar with the Northern tradition). Megin refers to a type of energy which is highly personalised. Your Megin will be very different from that of another; it is often thought of as the source of charisma in non-practitioners and as a type of spirituo-physical power in those who consciously wield it. You find Megin in nature as well as humans, and you find it in what we call souls or the energy bodies (Hamr), to be more exact. It is the power which drives all the manifestations of actual power. It is their fuel. In Northern lore we associate it with the 'power of Luck'. It is what fuels our luck, those oddities which happen in life from time to time to help us out, or in other terms 'spontaneous positive outflows of fate'. This power (Megin) is always highly confrontational (the Megin of one person will always clash with that of another, especially in any form of competitive or confrontational setting, even if it is something as simple as a negotiation). It radiates outwards from the individual, as this is often perceived by the 'subconscious' as charisma. When you meet someone and they just radiate a strong 'presence', you will have perceived their Megin (in the case of strong Megin-charged individuals). It affects not only the spiritual and energetic sides of things but also the physical – for instance, two athletes with exactly the same proficiency and physicality competing against each other would (providing everything else is on a par in between them) have the outcome decided purely on who had the most Megin. For our purposes, what interests us are its energetic and spiritual characteristics as Megin powers the manifestation and potential of our rune work.

In case you struggle with this concept, simply think of it as the fuel or power which powers your abilities and skills, your evolution of the Self. It has almost always a type of electric quality to it and is practically always of an electric blue energetic colour. The brighter and more vibrant this bluish tint, the more powerful its charge. The darker and duller, the weaker it is. Megin is always charged at a personal level – hence it is one of those universal energy types which do not have a positive or negative charge, but it is always uniform to the awareness which wields it. Megin was called Mana by the Austronesians[3]. For more information on Megin, see *The Breath of Oðin Awakens p.13*.

Now that we have Megin defined, we can look at the Hamingja. The simplest way to conceptualise the Hamingja is of it being a construct or rather an energy organ in the energy body (the Hamr – which is what we term the soul in our modern-day linguistics), which is responsible for the storage AND production of Megin. It is one of its primary functions. It gains an initial Megin charge at birth from our ancestral pools which last us until full maturity, at which point it typically runs at minimal levels until death. The whole point of learning about it and making active use of it is to enable us to produce greater quantities of Megin and direct its use according to our will. Typically, the Hamingja is situated on the back in between the shoulder blades (location-wise).

In Norse lore, the Eddas and Sagas contain numerous references to the Hamingja. Typically, it is referred to when being passed on to another (it is possible to send the Hamingja to support another with your luck/power for a limited time, or to gift it permanently to another upon your death) in the symbolic shape of a sword, or as a woman who joins herself to one of the heroes. Each time the Eddas tells of a gift of the sword, that is referring to the permanent passage of a Hamingja to another. See *The Breath of Oðin Awakens p.1* for more historical and theoretical information on the Hamingja. A quick side note here: many rune students have previously reported dreams of carrying a weight on their shoulders, a backpack or bag which is too heavy or takes too much effort to drag around and

Hamingja location on upper-back

is holding them back. That is a typical sign from your 'subconscious' that you have overcharged your Hamingja.

For our purposes, it is important for you to gain awareness of your own Hamingja, and learn how to fill it with energy, which will cause it to generate more Megin and then to extract that Megin from within it and put it to use in your rune work. This is going to be the primary focus on all the Hamingja practices given below.

Finally, having covered the Megin and Hamingja, we can look at what the Önd (in old Norse!) was referring to. A fun fact for you to illustrate just how linguistics can warp a concept over time, the modern-day Icelandic meaning of Önd is 'duck'! And I am told in Norwegian it means 'evil'. Very good examples how by changing a single word you warp the populations' understanding of important concepts into one of animalistic fun or one of dread. It becomes an 'Oh no, I must keep away from all that all at costs,' or the source of fun and jokes without anyone actually realising how important it originally was. Back to the matter at hand.

The Önd can be thought of as 'Megin-fuelled (or filled) breath'. Let us break this down a little. We know what Megin is since we have just discussed that above, but to understand Önd, we need to look at this concept of breath which can carry Megin. Naturally, it is not referring to normal breathing (although our usual breath also carries minute amounts of Megin). To understand this breath, you need to abstract your thinking a little and think of a human being as a Spark – we refer to this as the Spark of Self. This Spark is not a flame, yet it is often also thought of as a Seed, which technically speaking it is – the seed of a flame and potentially fire (in rare cases, a flame eventually becomes a sun).

This is the core of every life form, and from this Spark (which is found on the archetypal level of man) emerges the Spirit (Óðr) of that person. This then forms a body of fluidity about itself (giving you the energy body (Hamr)), which then solidifies into your physical body (Lik). In order to keep things alive, your core – or the Spark which you are on the archetypal level of existence – constantly sends out its energy (or light) throughout all the other parts of your Self. This flow of archetypal energy is this mysterious breath which Oðin gifted us all (through the original man, Ask and woman, Embla). Without this breath, there would be no flow and no transmission of essential manifestation-enabling (and life-enabling) energy for individualised Beings such as ourselves. If you think of trees in nature, they have a flow as well but that comes from the essence of nature flowing through the planet – in that case, it is a collective breath which gives life, whereas for mankind, it is an individual breath which gives life. This is why mankind moves away from collectives into individualisation when evolving. We are in effect evolving into our roots.

Think of the Breath of Oðin as the flow of archetypal energy from your core (your Spark or Seed), flowing through all parts of your Self and enlivening them. This is what the Önd's original actual meaning is and this what we will be using the term for. What flows through it is a very abstract type of Megin which we can add to, in order to amplify ALL its effects and further empower ourselves.

When in a physical body (Lik), the breath's Megin pool shifts from the Spark of Self into the Hamingja and the breath (or Megin charge flow) is inversed and flows from our bodies back into the Spark (Core) of the Self. This is how growth and life experiences are carried forth into our essences for it to grow, and the accumulation of those enhances it – which is one of the main purposes of life and how that tiny Seed/Spark can eventually mature into an actual Spark or Flame.

These basic overviews of the three concepts will give you a solid footing to understand when working with the initial practices. You are now ready to dive into the practical work! And have some proper fun!

Awakening the Hamingja

The strength or power of one's Hamingja is weakened due to its limited usage and lack of stress (or more correctly, friction). Using it – as most do – in a passive fashion and occasionally filling it with runic energy will not cause any degree of friction, which is needed to force it into action. Very much like a muscle in the physical body (Lik), if it is not exercised regularly or pushed, it will not grow, but will become subject to stasis and slumber.

The first step is to force growth. Fortunately, doing so is simplicity itself, as all parts of the Self want to and need to grow and evolve. Before delving into the exercises, you will need to establish contact with your Hamingja. Simply enter into a light meditative state, relaxing and allowing yourself to sink into a slight trance state. Having done so, feel the Hamingja as a type of container on your back; it sits in-between the shoulder blades and expands slightly downwards. Focus on it and will yourself to feel it. Will your perceptions of it to strengthen, focus awareness on it and send forth the desire to communicate. This is sufficient to raise a response. In case of difficulty, using the ᛖ Maður (Mannaz), ᚠ Óss (Ansuz) and ᚠ Fé (Fehu) combination of runes in sequence will assist in refocusing the sensing.

ᛖᚠᚠ

The manner in which this aspect of Self communicates with the conscious mind is the same way the 'subconscious' would, but is somewhat more instinctive. The Hamingja does not care about the wellbeing of the rest of the Self per se; it cares only about survival. Exercise your will to perceive and remain in a passive, receptive state of mind. Impressions will come through, in the form of a sensation or knowing, or an emotion. If there are unresolved issues, you will perceive a sensation of rejection, or a sense of 'I don't like you'. This too counts as a perception; it could be anger, aggression and so forth. All these negative impressions indicate that there is something to fix in the relationship; doing so requires an exchange of emotion. You just need to ask the Hamingja why it feels that way and project a sense of confusion towards it.

Communication in words or logical thought is only for the conscious mind, as the Hamingja uses a form of pure thought or rather intent to communicate. The important part of the previous instruction was the sense of 'confusion', which will be the part received by the Hamingja. The sense of confusion will prompt it to send a new sensation or emotion towards your conscious mind, which you will need to interpret and put into context in your conscious mode of thinking. Repeat this process until you have an idea of why it is feeling that way and then try to justify what has caused it by turning it into a new sensation you project back at it.

For instance, sometimes the Hamingja is angry because you might have harmed it. If the reason for your action was that you had no choice because you lacked understanding of the situation, or someone betrayed you and forced you to do something you did not want to or simply if you are sorry for that, project these impressions (or emotional senses) as you communicate with it. You will be amazed by just how much better you will start to feel once these nagging elements are resolved. Remember not to use just words, but attach the corresponding emotional or sensory response to these communications. As a matter of fact, words do not work, and we are so used to communicating in linguistic forms that we often forget that, in the grander scheme of things, language is a meaningless jumble of sounds. Words are empty (in most cases). 'Subconscious' elements of our selves do not recognise them in direct communications. Instead, in their attempts to do so, they will scan memories to identify what is related to the words, often with totally undesirable or unforeseeable results and misinterpretations.

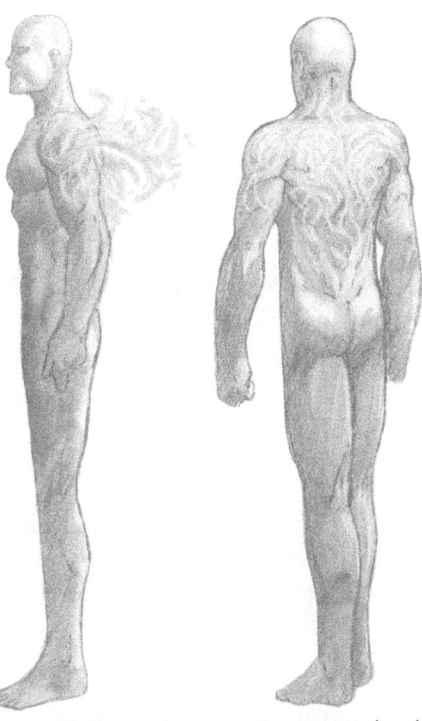

Hamingja location on upper-back

Quick Steps

1. Relax and enter into a meditative state.
2. Feel the Hamingja as a patch of energy on the back, in between your shoulder blades.
3. Focus in on it, feel it and let the intention to communicate with it arise.
4. Use the runes ᛘ Maður (Mannaz), ᚠ Óss (Ansuz) and ᚠ Fé (Fehu)
5. As you bathe in these runes' energies, remain perceptive and watchful for any impulse from the Hamingja.
6. Take note of sensations, impressions, feelings and emotions as they stir.
7. Respond, if you feel the need to, by sending a response in terms of an emotional or sensory message (as in you might feel the need to twitch, move, feel irritated, or feel completely at ease and so forth).

Having started to smooth out the relationship with the Hamingja, you are ready to focus on giving it a workout. Using Galdr or just uttering the ᚠ Fé (Fehu) rune whilst manipulating its energy is the starting point. This is what one can term the neutral energy for the Hamingja, its default, next would be the life force and finally your personal energy (an energy type unique to every individual).

Returning into a relaxed state, become aware of sitting in the middle of an incredible expanse, literally as if you were in the very middle of an infinite universe with nothing in it other than your Self. Utter the ᚠ Fé (Fehu) rune. Sit for a few moments, hearing the sound of the rune echoing in all that energy, feeling its heat and enjoying its red colour. With a firm perception of its energy, feel it as a prime runic energy. It is fundamentally linked to the first outpouring of Muspelheim, the first event from which other life springs forth. Let all this significance flow through the energy as a sensation, as a fundamental meaning. Slowly shift your awareness to the Hamingja on your back. Feel its boundaries and be within it. From this state of mind, focus on being within the Hamingja; with each in-breath, pull the fiery energies of ᚠ Fé (Fehu) into it. More and more, repeat this process of concentrating ᚠ Fé's (Fehu) energies into your Hamingja. Do so for a count of three breaths, then refocus on the ᚠ Fé (Fehu) energies outside of yourself and will them to fade gradually until none are left in the vast space about you, but maintain the concentrated ᚠ Fé (Fehu) energy that is in your Hamingja!

Slowly come out of the trance, becoming aware of your physical environment once more. You should feel the location where the Hamingja is slightly heavier. It can at times feel odd or annoying. Simply allow these sensations to pass. In case there is any serious disturbance, use the rune ᛦ Ýr (Elhaz) to strengthen the walls of the Hamingja and your auric field (see 'Hamingja for Protection' - The Breath of *Oðin Awakens, p.37*).

Quick Steps

1. Enter into a relaxed state.
2. Visualise yourself sitting in the middle of an infinite empty universe.
3. Utter the rune ᚠ Fé (Fehu), hearing its name echoing throughout the universe, seeing the burning red energy flood everywhere and feeling the heat.

4   Shift your awareness into the Hamingja (thick energy patch on your back, in between your shoulder blades).
5   From within the Hamingja, breathe in three breaths. As you do, visualise yourself breathing in not air, but the fiery red burning energy of the rune, which is all around you.
6   Shift your focus on the infinitely filled space around you and will that energy to fade away. Preserve what you have inhaled into the Hamingja; do not allow that to fade.
7   Gradually return to normal awareness by re-focusing on your immediate environment and your physical body (Lik).

Practice each and every day. Increase the number of breaths gradually by three, then six, then nine and finally twelve, at which point stop increasing them and instead make each breath deeper, pulling in more and more energy and condensing it (but making sure to avoid straining the breath while doing so).

At a certain point you will reach a cap, where taking in any more energy will cause discomfort. This is the indication that you have reached the current limit. It will grow with practice; no need to push too far too fast. The last thing you want is a fracturing of the Hamingja. Having to overuse ᛉ Ýr (Elhaz) in this case is a sign that you are overdoing it and risking damage. Just slow down, take a day or two to relax and allow the other parts of your Self to balance out. Knowing one's limit is of vital importance in this type of work, no matter whether one is dealing with the Hamingja, the High Galdr, the Fylgja or any other aspects thereof. Know your limits and push gently against them, a little each time, slowly and steadily, until they stretch and expand.

Here are some things you can keep an eye out for: as the Megin increases, the first sign will be a sense of wellness, of being alive. Gradually, a feeling of being re-energised will take hold, and physical health problems will typically start to smooth out. This is the first stage. After each practice, you will perceive a gradual type of sensation running about the surface of your skin. It is odd and difficult to describe: cool, yet not cold, giving off an electric type of buzz, but without being electric at all. For those who are able to, they will notice a clear difference between Megin and the life force; the two are essentially unmistakably different to the point where, having experienced Megin all over the body, it becomes impossible to ever confuse the two. The third sign of an increasing Megin pool and the quality of that pool is experiencing a sense of awe or something wonderful, which can be slightly intimidating to other people. A type of fearful or respectful distancing occurs from those who have interacted with the Megin, coupled with a distinct impression of difference that is 'subconsciously' perceived. It is very much like the "power of awfulness"[4] described by Marett when discussing the perceptibility of mana. These reactions are a good point to be aware of and to understand, but ultimately should be ignored as this reflects other people's reaction to the Megin. Eventually, as the Spark of Self starts to change the Megin, a type of attraction develops as others respond to the 'sense of greatness' from within. In any case, the increasing Megin pool will not go unnoticed – it simply cannot be. With that in mind, you will need to deal with the problem of being noticed by predators.

Awakening the Core of the Self

This is where things start to get exciting! At this point, the core dominant energy starts to be the energy used to fill the Hamingja. This will produce a specific type of Megin, which is unique to the Self as an individuated being. It is the ᛘ Maður (Mannaz) imprint of the Megin, which only you can produce. This special type of Megin is unique in creation; no other being will have the same type. It is a direct expression of the natural and the 'supernatural' (in fact, there is no such thing as 'supernatural', just aspects of the natural that are either not understood or not yet discovered) part of your Self. When working with this type of Megin and producing greater and greater quantities of it, a special ability is unlocked. This is best thought of as spontaneous event causation according to the individual will. Simply willing something to happen (providing one has the sufficient amount of this 'individualised' Megin) will cause it to take place. The more Megin available to spare, the faster events manifest. Even though this might all seem wonderful, and in some ways it is, but it does have an important downside as well: joking about things will have to be avoided at all costs, as will lying and deceit. Why? Because thoughts about something can unleash that into reality. In other words, telling a small lie such as not being able to make it into work for a day due to being 'sick' might have been a harmless thing to occasionally do before. At this point, however, such a thing will cause the illness to manifest within a very short time (and for some, it can virtually be that same day). In English, there is a good luck saying, which is 'break a leg'; it is a social linguistic play on words. However, for someone with this level of Megin, this expression would result in the person to whom these words are said actually breaking their leg. This is a good example of a completely innocent set of words with a humorous intent, which actually causes great harm. Wishing strangers 'good luck' is also to be avoided at all cost because it will spill some personal Megin over to them in order to bring forth that good luck.

Being aware of what one does, one says and one thinks, as well as what one feels at all times is the fundamental basis of living in the NOW. In this case, it is an essential component of staying safe and keeping the Megin pool charged.

A point to note is that, having started working with individualised Megin, the reserves of Megin should never, ever, EVER be allowed to drop too low. Why? Because being supercharged with unique Megin causes all seen and unseen beings to perceive it as a glowing sun in a dark universe; its amplification will, by its very nature, attract them like flies. Having a strong Hamingja with a fully charged pool of Megin stops them from being able to cause harm or drainage. However, allowing it to become empty gives rise to vulnerability. This is an effect of the strength of charge and does not require any additional work other than keeping the charge full.

Start by sitting in a relaxed position and sinking into a relaxed state of mind. Letting go of everything, allow the world to gradually fade away as the state of trance is induced.

Utter the following runes in this order: Sól, Perð, Fé, Þurs, Óss, Hagall, Maður, Óðal, Sól (for those of you using the Germanic names, the equivalents are: Sowilo, Pertho, Fehu, Thurisaz, Ansuz, Hagalaz, Mannaz, Othala, Sowilo), allowing their energies to flood the universe with you at its centre. With these runes, use the traditional red colours unless you are using High Galdr.

ᛋᚹᚠᚦᚨᚺᛗᛟᛋ

Having done so, relax and bathe in their energy, sound and vibration. What this runic chant does is to echo the experiences and potential of the Self stepping out of the Ginnungagap into individuation. Further information about this runic pattern will be given in a later publication, in order to avoid getting off course here.

Shift the focus into the personified Hamingja. Do not lose the awareness of the runic energies you have just called forth as you shift focus. Either breathe in that energy from the Hamingja or simply use your will to pull as much of it as possible without straining. Once the Hamingja's form is vibrating with this energy and no more can be taken in without strain, allow the runic energy to fade from the OUTSIDE, holding onto the energy inside of the Hamingja. Give it a few minutes to allow it to adapt to the energetic flow. Typically, you will feel a distinct energy rush; if not, you will sense a type of tension. Whichever it is, simply allow it to pass. Taking a few minutes for keeping still and enjoying this rush is a more than acceptable way to deal with integrating the new flow into the emerging Hamingja.

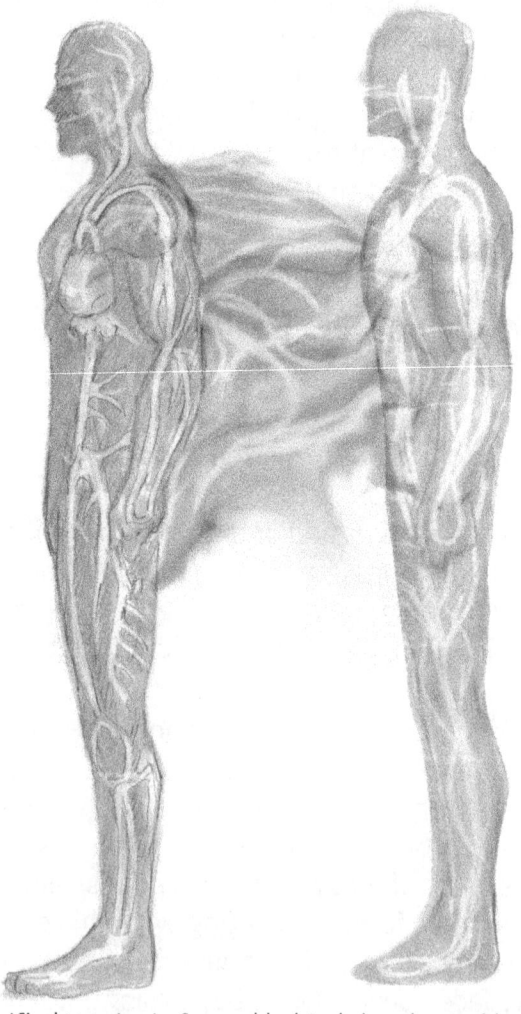

Personified Hamingja formed behind the physical body (Lik)

Once this newfound tension/rush has calmed down, allow all the energies to fade from your awareness (both within the Hamingja and within the universe at large). Next, utter the rune ᚠ Fé (Fehu) from within the Hamingja, feeling the burning rush of runic power only inside its form. This will cause a very special type of Megin to be produced. This version of Megin will not have the cool sensations of typical Megin, instead it will feel very unusual – a flowing, all-pervasive watery type. Enjoy the sensation; it is unique to this runic chant and only used in conjunction with it. As this Megin flows through the (personified) Hamingja, allow it to flow outwards and wrap it around yourself so that it resembles an auric field. Here again, allow the sensation(s) to pass after having acknowledged or enjoyed them, and observe the rune's energy fading away as well.

Quick Steps

1. Relax and allow the immediate surroundings and world to fade from awareness.
2. Visualise yourself sitting in a vast, empty space.
3. Chant the following runes (in this precise order): ᛋᚲᚠᚦᚱᚺᛗᛝᛋ and allow their energy to flood the space all around you (see Appendix A for correspondences).
4. Feel the energy, bathe in it, sense how it is a manifestation of the Self stepping out of the Great Nothingness and becoming something: that individualised 'something' that ultimately, down the generational lines, produced you.
5. Transfer your awareness into the Hamingja

by stepping into it and out of the physical body (Lik); stand behind it.
6. Either breathe into or pull into the Hamingja as much of this runic energy combination as you can without feeling any strain. Then allow whatever remains without to fade away (but not that which you have inside of it).
7. You should feel a rush; enjoy it and then allow it to naturally fade (without interfering with it).
8. Finally, from within the Hamingja, chant the ᚠ Fé (Fehu) rune, feeling its burning rush and tension radiate from the centre of the Hamingja outwards.
9. Step back into the physical body (Lik), and allow it to pull the Hamingja form and your awareness back into their respective places.

You have two choices: one is to simply step back into the physical body (Lik) and re-merge the personified Hamingja with it. The other is to use inner High Galdr and utter ᚠ Fé (Fehu) (only once) and then re-merge into the physical body (Lik). The former will allow your Hamingja in its own time to generate the Megin. In the latter case, it will force production to start immediately. If you use the latter approach, make sure you do not do any other Galdr (or meditation); simply focus on mundane tasks for the next few hours. You need to allow time to pass in order for the generation of Megin to take place uninterrupted.

This practice might seem complicated and intricate but do not allow this to dissuade you; with practice, it can take only a few minutes to perform effectively. It is essentially simple, once you get into the flow. It is a little more complex than the others since you are working in the realm of the Ásgarðians, specifically using techniques from Húnir (in other words, a higher consciousness way of doing things). It can be rather tricky when consciousness is not functioning at that level yet. Nonetheless, patience and practice will not only allow you to perform this within a few minutes, but doing so will start elevating your consciousness to that higher level. This practice combines a multitude of goals with one single practice: reaching higher consciousness, enhancing the Hamingja, expanding its capabilities, generating individualised Megin and developing the abilities for the instant casting of will into the worlds.

- Roadmap to High Galdr Rune Work -

Awakening the Breath of Oðin

This part of the practices is very exciting. It takes the theories and practical work of the Norse Self to a whole new level. Here is where we encounter the domain of Lóðurr's gift. Lóðurr, generally speaking, does not like being the centre of attention; he is the silent one (for good reason). All he asks in return for the knowledge given is to have it pointed out that he is neither Loki nor Freyr. Having fulfilled the promise to do so, it is time to focus on the practice at hand.

In this practice, we are going to be blending the personalised Hamingja with the physical body (Lik), whilst preserving a state of semi-independence in both. It is a very different practice from simply re-merging the Hamingja into the physical body (Lik). This has two direct effects: the first is to cause a permanent stretching of the Hamingja. It gains a solid elasticity, hence increasing the capacity for Megin storage and energy accumulation to what one can be forgiven for labelling a 'ridiculous' level. Second, it will cause the physical body (Lik) to be flooded with pure individualised

Megin. Imagine the boundary between the physical body (Lik) and the Hamingja blurring, where the blood of the physical merges with the Megin of the Hamingja. This causes the gifts of Lóðurr to awaken and activate.

Additionally, doing this will initiate a merging of the active 'subconscious' with conscious awareness. Senses become hyperactive, expanding your ability to sense a wider range of impressions than ever before. This involves a gradually and steadily awakening of the clair-senses – or more accurately, termed 'actual senses' rather than the restricted illusory ones that come as a default. As the Megin flows through the blood, it will activate the DNA; well, those parts of it that deal with the spiritual Self. You will notice 'your self' becoming more like the Self; expressing its actual nature will become second nature. The collective, the crowd and the masses will become more and more distant, and a gradual awakening of the Divine Self takes place. This practice is all about preparing the foundations for the full integration of all the parts of the Self into one uniform Divine Self.

Start by relaxing and going into a relaxed state of mind. Once relaxed, allow the world to fade out of your mind and into insignificance. Utter the rune ᚠ Óss (Ansuz). Allow its energy to flow through your body. Feel its vibrational power raising your consciousness and shifting it into a slightly ecstatic state, free from restriction, flowing, expanding and unlimited. Once you have reached that sensation of runic power, will it to fade completely.

Will the personified Hamingja to step out, with your awareness within it already. At this point, it will be like stepping out of your body yet still being within it. This automatic switch into dual-consciousness should

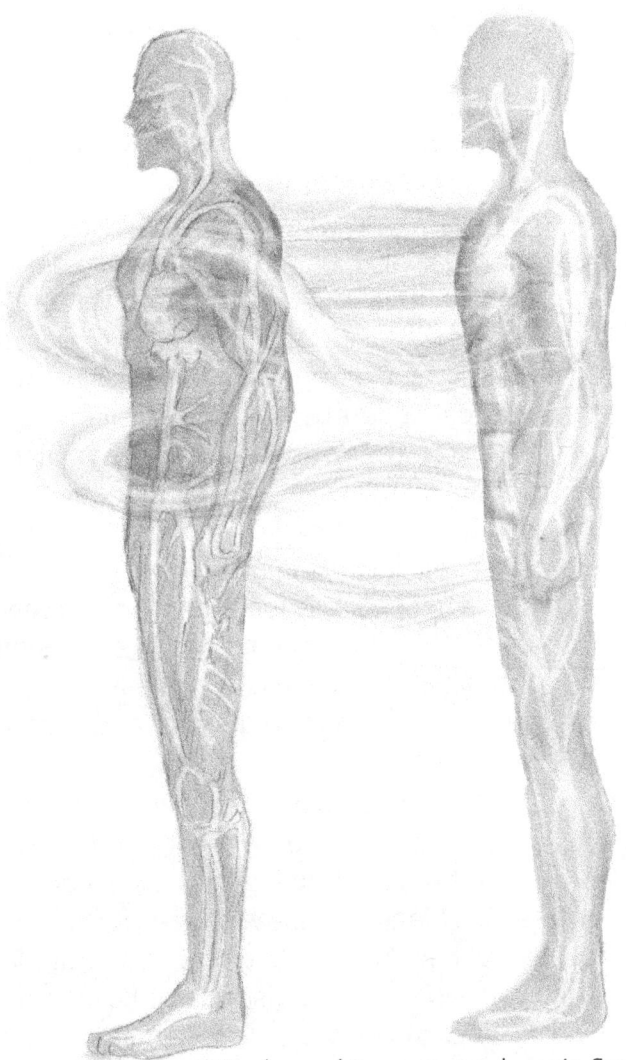

DNA charged & empowered megin flow
Hamingja to body and vice versa

require nothing more than a willed intent to achieve (providing your practice has been diligent up to this point). Focus in on the Hamingja and allow the sensory perceptions from it to flow; feel its form and its energies. Having done so, touch the physical body (Lik) and feel it as an external touch from the physical body's (Lik) perspective. Slowly and gradually, move in such a manner as to blend into the physical body (Lik). What is meant here is that the physical hands and arms will blend with the Hamingja's hands and arms, while the legs will be fused with the physical legs and so forth. The essential point is that the arms overlap with the arms, the legs with the legs, the torso with the torso, etc. If the one is slightly larger than the other, that is not a problem. Keep the awareness of both the Hamingja AND the physical separate; in this practice, the one does not fuse into the other; they are kept distinct but overlap. Your awareness should be of both forms simultaneously. This can be very confusing to begin with as the senses and the mind will become horribly muddled as to where each is functioning or perceiving from. Just relax and allow the temporary confusion to pass, keeping in mind that each of these forms is a source of sensory information distinct and separate, yet interconnected.

Once that has settled down, feel the surface of your physical skin. It should be easy to notice the Megin flowing all over it (as the Hamingja is now expanded all over it). Will this Megin to fuse with the physical blood and flow through it. At the same time, will that Megin to activate your DNA and energise it, as it flows through the blood. Relax and observe. It is impossible to describe the sensations or experiences this produces since they will be dictated by the DNA and by the individualised Megin. Whatever they are, relax and maintain the point of view of an observer taking notes but not reacting to them (or the trance can break). As the DNA activates, it creates an odd pulse. When this happens, will the pulse (and attached energy) to flow through the Megin back into the Hamingja. This causes a feedback loop.

In the first part, when the Megin flooded the blood, the Hamingja's essence flooded the physical. With the DNA's pulse, the reverse is taking place and the essence of the physical is flooding the Hamingja. This will bring the two systems into a harmonic state and spill over characteristics from the one into the other. Most importantly, this action will give the Hamingja a certain elasticity, and the physical body (Lik) as a container will help 'solidify' the Hamingja. This is an essential step to prepare it as a vehicle of Divine essence and consciousness.

To end the practice, simply focus on the Hamingja and will it to fuse with the physical body (Lik) as in previous practices.

Quick Steps

1 Start by relaxing and allowing the world to fade from your awareness.
2 Chant the rune ᚠ Óss (Ansuz); as you do so, feel the dark blue airy energy flow through your body, mind and awareness. Flow with it. If done correctly, a sense of freedom should gradually build up to the point where it gives rise to a thrill of the mind, an excitement, a form of ecstasy.
3 Step out of the physical body (Lik) in your Hamingja. Remember to shift your awareness into it until your sensory perceptions flow from it.
4 Using the Hamingja's hands, touch the physical body (Lik). This time, allow the Hamingja hands to blend into the physical hands. Make sure you keep them separate; do not allow

them to fuse into each other; instead, they should overlap while occupying the same space.
5. Keep making the two overlap into each other, Hamingja legs over physical legs, torso over torso and so forth until both forms are occupying the same space and overlapping. Since the Hamingja is energetic, it will flow a little further than the physical. It shimmers with an electric type of blue glow, which can stretch up to half an inch above the skin. In Jarls, it will be much more dominant.
6. Keep awareness, sensory input and consciousness separate; the training with receiving input from the two simultaneously, while remaining distinct, was preparation for this. Keep each one separate, even when they occupy the same space.
7. From the Hamingja, feel the surface of your skin on the physical body (Lik), then feel the skin from the physical body's (Lik) point of view. Notice the distinct sensation of Megin and remember it.
8. Will the Megin to flood the bloodstream (in the physical), fusing with it. Feel it, energise it and enliven it. As it does so, direct it to activate the DNA in your blood. If it helps, visualise and feel the double helix being flooded with the sparks of Megin, activating, enlivening and infusing. Take note of sensations, and notice the individualised energy and qualities from previous practices surface and vibrate through the bloodstream. This will create a strange pulse from the DNA throughout the blood. Take note.

9. Allow this pulse to strengthen. As it does, it emits the pulse into the flow of Megin in the streams of the Hamingja (equivalent to the blood capillaries, arteries and veins).
10. The flow of Megin should be from within the Hamingja into the physical body's (Lik) blood, activating the DNA, which pulses personalised Megin back into the Megin streams and Hamingja, harmonising the two and synchronising the flow of Self from the one to the other.
11. Repeat as many times as needed, until you are able to circulate and activate this synchronicity at will.
12. End the practice by merging the Hamingja's form into the physical body (Lik) by first separating from it, then merging in through the back as usual. Rinse and repeat this part until you can perform it without much effort.

The second stage is to get the core of the Self involved. Now the interesting part begins! Focus on your core (in the physical body (Lik)). Deep inside the solar plexus, sink until you reach centrality. This can be described as a sinking into the solar plexus, at a constant and flowing rate. The sinking produces a very deep, true trance state, and you need to be skilled at maintaining your functioning awareness of the physical body (Lik) whilst sinking into the core, which takes place. Practice as much as necessary. At one point during this sinking, something 'clicks' and you will encounter a clear feeling of all those characteristics of the core energy and Self previously identified. At the core, they can be described as pouring out of the 'sphere of the core' in the purest and subtlest manifestation. Having experienced this, the core Self has been touched; focus on it and will a merging (and sinking) of the conscious awareness into it. This is the Divine part of the Self; working with this will be covered in more detail later, for it allows the full expression of the 'God is within' mystery and the whole concept of the physical body (Lik) being a Temple to be brought into actuality.

For now, whilst maintaining awareness of the core and hence Spirit part of the Self, the physical body (Lik) AND the form of the Hamingja, will the Megin to spill from the Hamingja, through the blood and DNA, into the solar plexus and sink through it into the spirit realm of the Self until it reaches the core. This triple state of awareness is tricky to gain and even more difficult to maintain; do not rush it, be patient. Practice until it all 'clicks' into place. A quick note: once the core Self is reached, then providing the DNA and blood have been charged with Megin, the space around the core will pulsate with the individualised Megin. All that is needed is to pull it into the core itself. These perceptions, as well as the ability to maintain multi-levelled conscious awareness, take time. Do not despair; persistence pays off incredibly well here and results will come to those who put the effort in. It is also an excellent way to train the will!

Once the Megin starts flowing into the core, the Divine Spark at the very centre of the core will start to awaken and activate. It will become fierier and more dynamic (all Divine Sparks are fire-based, with no exception anywhere in creation; however, what they radiate is unique to each one of us). As it activates, it will pulsate energy rays as would a sun. Direct that out of the higher spirit realms via your solar plexus through the body and into the Hamingja. In case of difficulty here, simply switch the focus to the physical body (Lik) and feel those rays pulsating through the solar plexus whilst preserving awareness in the core and willing it to push the energy out through the solar plexus. Here, you are using the quantum point of the Self and, by acts of interaction, reshaping it and making it flow through the physical body (Lik). Those who are familiar with quantum physics will understand the concepts and probably be very surprised that they also apply to the Self within!

Quick Steps

1. Relax and let go of your surroundings.
2. Focus on your physical body (Lik), feel it, relax it. Shift your awareness to the midriff section of your body (commonly known as the solar plexus). It is an important intersection point for a multitude of nerve networks. In men, it is an even more important point because it is the central point of gravity of the physical form, hence also the central point of one's entire Self.
3. Visualise yourself inside that point, see, feel and sense from that point outwards. Once settled in that point, sink and allow yourself to go deeper and deeper. Keep on sinking. This will produce a deep trance. Keep on sinking, deeper and deeper, until you feel a type of 'click'. It should be either proceeded or followed by a strong sense of the qualities of your Self (as identified in the previous work).
4. Sink into this sense of characteristics as

they radiate outward. You will find yourself in the centre of the Self. Feel it radiating the characteristics of YOUR Self; sense it, get to know it.

5. Maintaining focus inside your core, expand your awareness so that you also become aware of your physical body (Lik), then add to that an awareness of the Hamingja as it overlaps the physical. Spend a couple of minutes strengthening and re-establishing this triple synchronous awareness. Having gained a firm grip of this threefold awareness, expand the physical to include not only the Hamingja but also the Megin flowing through it. Then, will it to flow into the physical blood (Lik) and DNA. Remember to keep the threefold awareness; you MUST not lose focus of all that whilst expanding into the blood, DNA and Megin.

6. As the DNA gets activated with Megin and starts to pulse, feel it growing stronger and stronger until its pulse flows back through the physical body (Lik) into the space where the Spark of Self is. Let the pulse flow inwards towards you as you are in the centre of the Spark of Self. As it touches the Spark, pull it in; if it helps, see yourself 'breathing' in that pulse's energy.

7. As this energy enters the Spark of Self, it will burst into hyperactivity and start to radiate out in a series of Megin-charged pulses of Self. These will be noticeably different from the previous one. How so depends entirely on your Self, making it impossible to describe.

8. As it pulses outwards, it will flow out of the

solar plexus then throughout your physical body (Lik), back through the bloodstream into the Hamingja.
9   This completes one breath. Increase by one breath each time you want to increase the effects of this practice. At three complete breath cycles, you will be ready to move on. To end this, simply re-merge the Hamingja form with the physical body (Lik) and return to your daily life.

Having made this energy actually flow from the outer into the inner and then from the inner into the outer (blood and DNA into the core and then from the core back out through the solar plexus into the blood and DNA, then spilling into the Megin in the Hamingja), you will notice a very empowering and distinctive effect, which will become obvious to the whole totality of your Being. Details are unnecessary here; results speak for themselves. All that is worth saying is that the Divine Self surfaces into the world and in each and every one of these breaths and subsequent actions. In other words, the Megin-fuelled breath (Önd) starts to flow. Blessed be the Breath of Oðin within!

This is what the Breath of Oðin actually is; the flow of Megin, personalised by the DNA and the Self's core, flowing through the physical, Hamingja and Spirit of the individual. It is both the flow and what flows, the substance and the function (in other words, the characteristics of this energy combined with its power, set in motion during an in-flow and out-flow motion). It is also at times referred to as: Megin-fuelled or Megin-filled breath.

Regardless of how long it takes to master this practice, it is damn well worth doing until you have fully mastered it. It is the second step to fully awakening the Divine within. If you look back over the practices so far, you will notice that the Hamingja has now awoken and become active; the DNA is activated and individualised Megin flows through the two and the physical body (Lik), which subsequently flows into the core of the Self. The core pulses out the Breath of Oðin, which in turn flows from that most mysterious place in the spirit realm of the Self, back through the physical body (Lik), merging with the Megin and empowering the Hamingja. The final piece of the puzzle to a fully awoken Divine consciousness is the addition of the merging of the geometric (or animal-human formed) Fylgja, for which this is the preparatory process.

Keep increasing the individualised Megin, and keep working on making it flow through the physical body (Lik) into the core Self and making the Breath of Oðin flow from the core of the Self through the physical, merging with the Megin and flowing into the Hamingja's form as new, divinely empowered Megin. If it is the only thing you ever do, master this well. It is THAT important. The final step will be covered in the geometric Fylgja teachings but for it to function, this divinely empowered individualised Megin is needed first.

ESSENTIAL PRACTICES FROM THE SPIRIT OF HÚNIR AWAKENS

Key Work From The Spirit of Húnir Awakens

In this section, you will be working on the next level of your Self (and level in creation), namely the mental or spiritual (they are technically speaking one and the same as the mental is a perception of the spiritual – in other words, the mind (Hugr) is a manifestation or product of the Spirit (Óðr)). Here, you will undertake key practices and learn key concepts extracted from *The Spirit of Húnir Awakens (Parts 1 & 2)*. Unfortunately, those titles are quite extensive, including just under 500 pages (in total) of material to cover. Here you will find only the most minimal and essential information you need to develop in order to move onto actual High Galdr, but I would recommend taking the time to pick up those titles and work through them at some point because the fundamentals they provide are often the missing instructions in other works, which result in many stumbling blocks people have in general practical work.

Here we will be looking at the second gift made by Húnir (or in some texts he is referred to as Ville when they talk about the holy trinity of gods: Oðin, Ville, Ve).

That gift to Ask and Embla was Spirit (Óðr), out of which manifested Mind (Hugr) and Memory (Minni) (typically symbolically referred to as the two Ravens of Oðin).

From this section's work, I would strongly suggest working through things in the order in which they are presented. This is most important because the whole goal of all *The Spirit of Húnir Awakens* work is to widen your perceptual scope a little at a time with each practice. Skipping one of them will leave you unable to fully grasp the next. This problem is entirely avoided when doing them in the correct order. Pay special attention to the becoming conscious of your Spirit (Óðr), enhancing the senses, and Spirit (Óðr)-shaping practices. Those abilities are critical for ALL the work you will undertake here and in all later practices. The shaping into runes can be tricky, so I would suggest taking those slowly, one rune at a time, as an ongoing work in progress. In other words, you can do that one (providing you keep on doing it until you complete ALL the runes) as you move on. You do not need to wait to complete all those runes before progressing further. The work with the Hugr Raven is important but not as critical to preparatory work as the Spirit (Óðr). As long as you do it, there is no need to try and develop deep mastery in it at this stage, unless of course you want to. We are not including the Minni Raven work, as that is mainly used for developing the Self and advanced Galdr. If you want to cover that, I would suggest picking up a copy of *The Spirit of Húnir Awakens (Part II)*.

The important point is to remember all this is about extending your conscious control and awareness into the realm of your Spirit (Óðr). Consciousness is a by-product of physicality and as such it has to be stretched and made more subtle in order to be able to function at this level (and potentially at even higher levels of creation and the Self).

Here you will be taking those steps in a firm and decisive manner and notice that as your consciousness and its reach expand, so do your awareness and perceptions.

- Roadmap to High Galdr Rune Work -

Understanding the Óðr, Hugr and Minni

As with the previous section, here come into play a few key terms which need to be understood in order to be able to maximise the practical side of things. First and foremost is the Óðr, which can be thought of as Spirit. This term is quite a good fit – albeit not a perfect one – to the meaning of Óðr. If you prefer to, you can think of Spirit as a good term for Óðr, but our modern-day understanding of what spirit actually represents is very limited.

Let us look a little more in depth at what its actual meaning refers to. The most precise definition of Óðr is an outpouring (or outreaching) of the core of the Self basically, the outwards radiation of the emanations of the Spark of Self. Apologies for the high level of abstraction here, but unfortunately it is simply not possible to convey the actual meaning in layman's terminology. This reaching out is manifested via means of perception – and hence the senses, as the main perceptual tools available to mankind at this point in time. The expansion of this reaching out of the Self via perceptual mechanisms allows our Self (Spark) to grow and this in turn is the foundation of awareness, as the new perceptions are processed via the Hugr and subsequently recorded in the Minni. The functions of the Hugr then give rise to consciousness, which results in conscious awareness and intellectual capabilities arising out of the entire process.

Deeper Insights
Into Actual Óðr

So far, we have looked at some of the characteristics of the Spirit (Óðr) such as abstracted awareness, and its equivalence to what we understand as spirit in our modern-day terminology and inspiration. Let us now look at an over-arching conceptualisation of what the Spirit (Óðr) actually is.

Very much like the Megin-filled breath (Önd), it is an active principle, one governed by action and reaction. It is not a container or embodiment part of the Self but rather can be thought of as a flow of some type. Naturally, this will give rise to the question: A flow of what? To answer that, we need to come to a definition of what Spirit (Óðr) is. The two are basically the same question: one in Old Norse concepts and the other in modern-day. Since the Spark of Self is a totally individualised expression of some part of the Divine, it gains motion. This motion is carried back and forth via the Megin-filled breath (Önd). The Spirit (Óðr) is the next stage of this process. As the Breath carries these characteristics of the Self forth, the Spirit (Óðr) coalesces into an expression of some or all of them. Metaphors typically assist with the description of these complex abstractions.

Picture, if you will, a spark and imagine that its characteristics (how it shines, what it is made of, its purpose, its uniqueness, etc.) are being carried in all directions by the Megin-filled breath (Önd). As this Breath turns, twists and swirls about, it splits into multiple flows of energy and, at certain points, it will interact with itself, crossing over a previous flow, merging with another and so forth. These events will cause a concentration of the breath to form, or if you prefer, a small 'blob' of breath energy. Those are what cause the Spirit (Óðr) to be. The requirements for Spirit (Óðr) formation are naturally more complex than this, but the underlying principle can be grasped by this simplification. What Húnir did when he bestowed Spirit (Óðr) is to cause the flow of breath bestowed by Oðin to turn twice, causing an eventual merge into a massive formation, which was the initial Spirit (Óðr). Lóðurr's work comes after for a good reason. Húnir could not have achieved this formation of Spirit (Óðr) unless Oðin had already bestowed the Megin-filled breath (Önd) on Ash and Embla – he needed the flowing breath. Likewise, Lóðurr's shaping could not occur without Húnir having formed the Spirit (Óðr).

The key requirements for formation of Spirit (Óðr) are yet again threefold. The initial breath contains essence of the Spark of Self, hence we have activity – it flows! The principle of heat (outwards flow) is present, hence the masculine is manifest. With the manipulation and motion of that flow, the airy principle is born, hence the feminine is manifest. Then under the direction of Húnir, the coalescing of these flows takes place and the principle of attraction is born, along with sensing, both water principles (which in the Norse tradition, as well as Greek and Roman, are masculine) bring us back to the masculine. We will cover polarities and cosmic polarities at a later point in time. Remember, water is melted ice and carries the life principle (fire) within it (hint: in Norse mythology, as in Greek mythology, the God of the Sea is male (those being: Njörðr and Poseidon respectively)).

Once these three principles are brought together, we have manifestation at a very abstract level but manifestation nonetheless. This is one of the symbolic meanings hinted at by the triangles in the Valknut (the Norse triple-triangle symbol). Keep in mind, too, that the triangle is a three-sided and four-pointed polygon (including the central point!).

- Roadmap to High Galdr Rune Work -

The Hugr and Minni: Functional Manifestations of the Óðr

It is now time to look at how the Spirit (Óðr) relates to the Minni (which we can, for the time being, think of as memory) and Hugr (think of it as mind, reason or logic). As it forms out of a dual polarity, one masculine and active, the other feminine, contractive and receptive, it gains characteristics of both. Once fully formed, the Spirit (Óðr) itself manifests primarily through those two poles and their interaction. These are then isolated in dominant manifestations which give rise to the mind-reason (Hugr) and Minni. The mind-reason (Hugr) is the primarily active part of the spirit's (Óðr) functions and the Minni is the formative/cohesive one. It is important to keep in mind that since these are manifestations of characteristics of the Spirit (Óðr), they are no longer pure. You can get a passively functioning Hugr (what we produce when entering into trance states, prior to switching to a higher form of conscious perception) as well as an active element to the Minni. It typically functions passively, building and activating memories without conscious interference, BUT you can also actively join the memory processes and stir them consciously. It follows perfectly the principles of manifesting polarities, where each pole will always contain various degrees of its anti-pole.

Understanding the Hugr and the Minni should at this point start becoming easier. We have seen how the Spirit (Óðr) expresses the Strong and Weak Nuclear Forces and how the former is manifested in the Hugr and the latter in the Minni. It is no wonder they are represented in the symbolic language as the Twin Ravens of Oðin. The form of birds represents a constant flow of activity, a pushing forth and back, a freedom from bindings and so forth. Interestingly, using the Raven as the symbolic bird for the expression of these parts of the Self gives us further insight into what our ancestors actually knew about the Hugr and Minni. The Raven is typically used as the bird which is able to pass between the realm of the living and the dead. In other words, it can move between the states of living activity and the passivity of death, the bursting forth of new life (active-masculine) and the passivity and approach of stasis (passive-feminine), the investigatory analytical experiential and the record-keeping solidifying and so forth. Note that here we are looking at the two polarities expressed on the mental level of reality, not others (at least not yet).

The neutral element (electromagnetic force) is what interlinks the two and builds an interdependence. It allows the experiential activity of the mind-reason (Hugr) to be recorded by the Minni, as well as work in the opposing direction where the memories from the Fylgja flow through the Minni (or the Minni's memory stores) to be accessed by the mind-reason (Hugr) for analysis and experiencing.

Please note the Fylgja and the Minni are covered in detail in other books as they are not required pre-requisites for learning High Galdr, which is what we are aiming for here.

Mind, Spirit or Spirit-Mind
Unveiling the Hugr

The very concept of mind and what it is has plagued human understanding ever since it was first introduced. So many debates about where the mind is in the brain (or was it the heart?), whether mind was spirit, etc. have all gone unresolved. Even modern-day psychologists and the neurosciences are unable to pinpoint what the mind actually is or where it resides with any certain precision.

For us, this is a total non-issue. The Spirit (Óðr) is ultimately non-physical and not subject to the laws of space. Therefore, trying to pinpoint its location is a fool's errand. It is nowhere and everywhere due to not being subject to space or time. The mind, on the other hand, is a product of the Hugr's functioning, hence one could loosely equate the two. Additionally, if your definition of the mind includes memory, then it would be a product of the functioning of both the Hugr and the Minni. Since we know where each of those parts of the Self ground themselves (namely the cortex and left side of the brain for the Hugr and the cerebellum and the right side for the Minni), the mind is firmly rooted in the brain.

As for the heart, well, it simply does not belong anywhere in the equation. These days, far too much emphasis and importance are being placed on the heart, even going so far as suggesting that it is THE primary energy centre of the entire person. This could not be further from the truth! Anyone who can see or sense energy will know that the heart is nothing more than the reflection of the Spark of Self (an agent, if you like). The primary energy centre of the person is actually the solar plexus, not the heart, and it is from that centre that energy is circulated throughout all the parts of the Self. It should be noted that modern-day sciences have found that the heart does generate an electromagnetic field stronger than that of the brain, which might seem to contradict the above. It does not, however, for the reason that this stronger field is due to the circulating blood flowing through the heart and the vast amount of neural presences there. these relate to biological awareness not Spirit (Óðr) As we will see later, where consciousness focuses, blood flow and neural activity increases. Now what would happen if you actually constantly had it in the heart region? It would all over-develop. Energetic overdevelopment in this region causes vulnerability to and reliance on emotion. The modern-day unhealthy obsession with love stems from such over-development, where some people simply break down when they believe they are lacking love. It also accounts for all the unstable bursts of emotion which are all too common these days.

Becoming Conscious of the Óðr (Spirit)

Gaining conscious awareness of the Spirit (Óðr) is not difficult; it just requires a little patience and practice. In order to do so, you need to gain a sense of the energy body (Hamr) first, and from it the Spirit (Óðr) is perceived directly.

Simply sit in a comfortable position and relax, allow the world to fade for a while as you let go of all tension and worries. Just breathe and relax. As you are sitting, keep perfectly still and try not to move the body (Lik) at all. Instead, become aware of your skin – all of it. This should be a fairly simple task but if you struggle, fixate on one arm, then add the other, then the head and face and so forth. The idea is to gradually build up until you can maintain the sense of your skin all over your body. If you have no issues, perfect! Time to move on.

While keeping your skin in focus, visualise the space inside of the skin as empty. You are blanking out the organs, muscles, bones and so forth. All you want in your awareness is your skin and nothing within it. Since you have your eyes closed, the next step is to focus on looking straight ahead BUT KEEPING THE EYES CLOSED. You should 'see' blackness in front of you. As you do, realise that your point of view is behind your eyes staring out through them into the blackness of your eyelids. If you see energy blobs or waves, just ignore

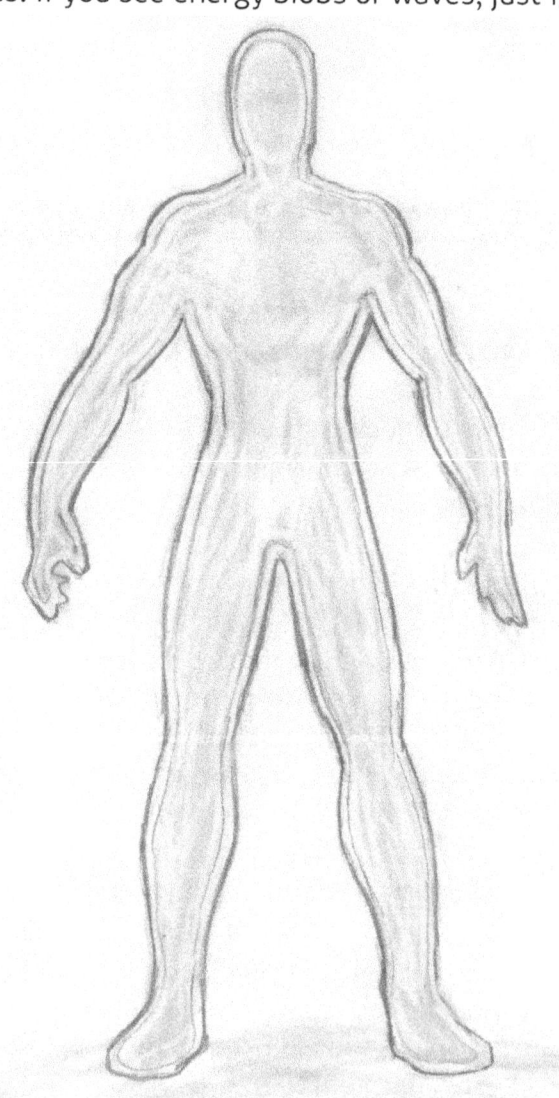

Spirit (Óðr) inside the energy body (Hamr)
inside physical body (Lik)

them – they are nothing more than the electric effect of neural firing at the back of the eyes. Once this clicks into place, extend it so that you feel yourself inside the skin just as you are inside the eyes, as if you are sitting just under the skin as well as behind the eyes. This is the peripheral sensing of the energy body (Hamr) which we will focus on in the next title.

Once all this is firmly grasped, the next and final move is to feel what is on yet another deeper layer. In effect, if you think of Russian nesting dolls which fit inside one another, it works well in this context. You are inside your physical skin (Lik), which is the energy body (Hamr). When you are inside the Hamr, that is the peripheral Spirit (Óðr). This is what you are aiming for. Unlike the physical body (Lik) and energy body (Hamr), the Spirit (Óðr) only has shape because it is contained – in actuality it has no fixed shape per se but being in a physical body and in an energetic one, it gains form. The more you practice holding onto the perceptions of the Spirit (Óðr) being inside the energy body (Hamr) (think of it like a suit) and the energy body (Hamr) being inside the physical (Lik), you will solidify your sense of the Spirit (Óðr).

It is worth spending a while becoming familiar with what it is like to be feeling from the Spirit (Óðr) through the energy body (Hamr) and finally into the physical (Lik). With a little practice, you can switch to being fully grounded in the Spirit (Óðr) within a fraction of a second. It becomes pretty much a reflex which takes nothing more than a single thought.

When you have a good sense of the Spirit (Óðr), meditate on the fact that this is YOU, that it is a direct manifestation of your Spark of Self. Keep the focus within. You might sense it being present beyond the confines of the physical (Lik) and energy bodies (Hamr), but do not worry about it too much as that is just the mental auric field. We will use that later on, but for now, the important part is becoming aware of the Spirit (Óðr) and being able to switch back to it with as little trouble as possible. Naturally, as with all things, the more often you do so, the easier this will become.

When you are ready to end the practice, refocus on the energy body (Hamr) whilst allowing the sense of the Spirit (Óðr) to gradually fade, then do the same with the energy body (Hamr), allowing it to fade as you refocus on the physical (Lik). Each time, move outwards from level to level until you hit the physical (outermost). When you have reached the physical, run your awareness along the skin of your body and slowly get out of trance.

Quick Steps

1. Sit comfortably and relax, allowing the world around you to fade away for a while.
2. Be perfectly still and do not move physically.
3. Expand your sense of feeling across all the skin of your body, feeling all of your skin over every inch of your body. If you struggle, start with one arm, then two, then add the legs and so forth until you can get it all.
4. Visualise the space inside the skin as being empty – no organs, no blood, just emptiness.
5. Shift to your sight, keeping your eyes closed and looking straight ahead. See the blackness there and lock into that position. Try not to move the eyes at all, once you get them looking straight ahead. Feel yourself looking out from behind your eyes.

6. Now feel yourself sitting behind your skin on the inside of it AND behind your eyes.
7. Next, expand that feeling of being inside to a third layer, so you are inside your skin (that being the energy body (Hamr)), and then subsequently inside the energy body (Hamr). Put in as much practice as needed. It will simply click into place at a certain point. That is what it feels like to be within and aware of your Spirit (Óðr).
8. Once you have it, simply remain aware of it and reflect on the fact that this is the actual manifestation of YOU. It sits nicely inside the confines of the shape of your energy body (Hamr), which in turn is cosily tucked within the physical (Lik).
9. When done, simply refocus on your physical body (Lik) by first shifting focus to the energy body (Hamr) (so you are losing one layer in your perceptions) and now are just inside the skin of your physical (Lik). Then shift to the physical body (Lik) itself. Take a deep breath and return to your normal awareness.

Doing this teaches various parts of your Self, especially the conscious part, how to shift from one layer of the Self to the next and back. When aware of the physical body (Lik), you are within the physical layer of energetic reality. When aware of the energy body (Hamr), you are at the pure energetic layer of reality and finally, when aware of the Spirit (Óðr), you are at the mental layer of reality. We will look at how to reach the others later on. For now, suffice it to master these three (physical, energetic and mental). Practice often, as this is yet another one of those cornerstone skills you need for all further work.

Roadmap to High Galdr Rune Work

Spirit and Senses, Awakening and Development

This is an extension of the previous practice. It aims to not only bring the sensing of the Spirit (Óðr) forth but also the perceptions of the actual five senses as they function. You will need at least a reasonably good level of skill on the previous practice to do these ones.

With this, you will start by becoming aware of the Spirit (Óðr) as explained in the previous exercise. Once the sensation of being inside the physical (Lik) as the energy body (Hamr) and then inside the energy body (Hamr) as the Spirit (Óðr) is firmly set as consistently as possible, shift your focus to your ears. When you hear a sound, it is picked up by the physical ear but since you are also inside the physical, your energy body's (Hamr) ear will pick it up and drive the sound to the 'ear' within the Spirit (Óðr). Remember, you will have shifted your conscious awareness inside the Spirit (Óðr) so it makes sense that the ears of the Spirit (Óðr) are processing what is being heard. Practice this as often as possible. Becoming aware of how the Spirit (Óðr) processes the incoming sensory input is not only critical to future advanced work but will provide you with many useful skills and abilities. The most important benefit in this day and age is that it also prevents subliminal messages from being processed. As soon as the Spirit (Óðr) processes meaning, consciousness can accept or reject things directly. The other extremely important effect of sensory processing by the Spirit (Óðr) is that eventually, you will not be limited to only what you can physically see, hear, feel and so forth. Reading energies, perceptual expansion and many more advantages will open up quite naturally to a trained Spirit (Óðr). Eventually you will even start to perceive the pure conceptual thoughts behind whatever your senses pick up. This is when you will in effect 'wake up' the Spirit (Óðr) fully (we will call this process 'shifting into the Óðr', for future reference). Needless to say that when this awakening takes place, a phenomenal expansion of each and every part of the Self occurs.

Once you have gained a good grasp of hearing from the Spirit (Óðr), do the same with touch, then taste and smell. Leave sight for last. Why? Because we are so bound up in seeing in our physical environment that the other senses fall behind. By training them first and foremost, you will have equalised the senses as you activate them at the Spirit (Óðr) level, rather than having to work harder on those which have been left behind. Naturally, we all struggle with some and find the others easy – that is to be expected – do not be discouraged by it! Just work through the weaker ones.

Quick Steps

1. Become conscious of the Spirit (Óðr) (as outlined above).

2. Focus on your ears from the point of view of being within your Spirit (Óðr).
3. Concentrate on what you hear. Each time you hear something, notice that you are not only just hearing through the physical ears but that your energy body's (Hamr's) ears are picking up the sound wave of whatever it is you are hearing. Then focus on the fact that as it does, your Spirit (Óðr) picks up that vibration of sound and attaches context, meaning, or significance to it. It is where your conscious awareness processes what is heard.
4. When able to easily do this with hearing, switch to one of the other senses until you have mastered them all.

Using Óðr Directly From Within the Physical

Being aware of the Spirit (Óðr) and becoming aware of its functioning in your daily life is a progressive yet critically important skill that you should be working on as much as possible. When you speak, listen, see and react to the world around you, when you observe your own experiences, emotions, feelings and so forth, it is then that being aware that they shift from the physical or emotional to the Spirit (Óðr) and being conscious of the responses from the Spirit (Óðr) is essential. Developing this perceptual widening will be a boon in many of the forthcoming practices, eventually leading to an awakening of Spirit (Óðr) awareness, which in turn eventually leads to full awareness and to actions from the Spark of Self.

Awakening Higher Levels of Sensory Perception

When a good solid working of the senses at the Spirit (Óðr) level has been developed, we can take that foundation and expand on it by what can be termed hyper-evolving the senses. This is achieved by runic work in conjunction with the above sensory practices.

It is all very simple to do once the former has been mastered. When you are listening with your Spirit (Óðr) ears, chant the ᚠ Óss (Ansuz) rune. See the dark blue energy explode all around you, feel the air flow and lightness, hear the name of the rune echoing everywhere. Having done so, refocus on hearing from within the Spirit (Óðr) and listen to the ᚠ Óss (Ansuz) energy. As the senses carry it through the physical (Lik) and the energy body (Hamr) to the Spirit (Óðr), feel how they carry the energy of the rune. As you keep focussing on it and on hearing it from the Spirit (Óðr), will the hearing to amplify become more powerful and more precise; will its reach to expand. After doing this for a while, you will notice the spirit's (Óðr) sense of hearing change and expand. It will not only become easier but will start to carry more information to you. It will no longer be just the sound; it will also include information. Do not worry about 'decoding' or understanding that information just yet, as that would distract you. At this point, all you want to do is keep expanding the sensory capabilities and your grasp of listening from within the Spirit (Óðr). When done, will the ᚨ Óss (Ansuz) energy to gradually fade away. When it has gone, you should no longer hear, feel or see it. Now refocus on your hearing in the Spirit (Óðr) once more before you shift out of trance and back to your physical Self (Lik).

Quick Steps

1. Follow the previous practice to focus in on perceiving (start off with hearing) from the Spirit (Óðr).
2. Once you have a good sense of it, chant the rune ᚨ Óss (Ansuz). See the dark blue energy exploding all around you, feel the air flow and the lightness of the energy, hear the name of this rune echoing within and throughout this energy.
3. As you hear through the physical body (Lik), into the energy body (Hamr) and finally in the Spirit (Óðr), focus on its sound, vibration and feeling.
4. When it reaches the spirit's (Óðr) hearing, it will change it, enhance it and amplify its ability to hear throughout the three levels (on the archetypal level via the Fylgja) on the mental/spiritual (via the Óðr), on the energetic (via the Hamr) including the physical (via the Lik)).

You will notice over time that your physical sense of hearing will also increase as a side effect of this practice. It may also potentially produce minor awakenings in energy body (Hamr) hearing. Do not worry about those for now as we will focus on the energy body (Hamr) elsewhere; just do not think you are going insane if you pick up a voice or sound where there is no physical source for it. If it bothers you, simply refocus on your physical ears and will it so that only the information received by them is carried into your awareness at this point in time. By doing this, you can actually develop the ability to switch on or off hearing at any level of your Self. This is highly recommended! Just remember to refocus on the ears when you do the practice again and will them to carry any information from those sources to your awareness at that point! If you are going to switch off, you will need to switch on when needed before practising and then of course switch off again, once you are done.

The same practice is repeated with the other senses – just switch to the relevant sensory organ and use the runes which activate it as follows:

Hearing: ᚠ Óss (Ansuz) and ears. Colours: dark blue with a sensation of ease
Sight: ᛋ Sól (Sowilo) and eyes. Colours: white with a sensation of heat but not burning
Touch: ᛚ Lögur (Laguz) and skin. Colours: blue-green with a cool sensation
Taste: ᛃ Ár (Jera) . Colours: darker yellow with a sensation of dry weight
Smell: ᚷ Gjöf (Gebo) . Colours: dark blue with a sensation of moist air

Having perfected the senses one at a time, proceed to combining two in one practice session, then three, then four, and so on, until you are able to have all five active at once. When combining them, focus on sight first, then hearing, then touch/feeling, and only then add taste or smell in whichever order you wish. Do not neglect any one of the senses or the sixth sense will always elude you. More on the sixth later on.

Remember that it is important to avoid falling into the trap of sight. We tend to be so reliant on sight that the function of other senses is subdued, if not completely ignored. For instance, when walking in town, do you notice the scents about you? The feeling of the space about you, the floor you are walking on? Do you hear the thousands upon thousands of sounds? Recall how as a child you would put everything in your mouth. You had to taste the pencil, touch it, play with it, bang it against the table, throw it about. All these actions involved gathering a huge amount of sensory data in comparison to what adults do. In that manner, the perceptions of the child are far superior to that of the adult. Try to involve as many senses as possible in your perceptions. Within reason of course – no one is suggesting going around tasting the pavement you are walking on! Throw away those plastic and rubber shoes and get proper ones that allow the sensory receptors of your feet to pick up the solidity of the floor you are walking on – they cannot pick up such sensations through rubber, gels, and plastics because those are isolators. Let your sense of smell go wild, expand your feeling to feel the space you are walking through and only then focus on sight. Experience everything as fully as you can with your basic tools of perception! Then expand it into Spirit (Óðr) sensing. You will discover that suddenly, you are aware of an entire world of information that you had no idea was there. Throw away those damn mobile phones, unbind yourself from those interruptions, and set yourself free!

Roadmap to High Galdr Rune Work

The Óðr and Shaping the Spirit

Having developed sensing from within the Spirit (Óðr) the next step can be taken – reshaping the Spirit (Óðr)! As we have briefly looked at above, it is not really bound to shape but only conforms to a shape because the energy body (Hamr) dictates it via the physical body (Lik). As far as the Spirit (Óðr) itself is concerned, it is more of a flow or active set of manifest concepts of the Self. **In other words, it is a shapeless abstraction.** However due to the limitations of our awareness, humans and most life forms are unable to deal with such levels of abstraction directly and thus start from the basis of shape and gradually, as we evolve, move closer towards that abstraction and the perceptions thereof.

Due to the limitations of shape, our shapes dictate our perception and awareness, as well as our modes of thinking. When we want to reshape, we have to change our way of thinking and its scope. This is what we are going to start working on now. One of the big gains (and just how big cannot be stressed enough) with this practice is a loosening of the bonds of flesh upon our conscious awareness. As we reshape, we shift our consciousness, transpose the awareness and change our modes and scopes of thinking. This is not a new practice; it has been used in more limited forms in other cultures, but the Norse are its greatest adepts. Lady Freya, Oðin and even Loki are often described in the Eddas as shifting forms. The Berserker warriors do so, albeit only partially, and the Seidr women shift into their Fylgja forms and so forth. This is pretty much an all-encompassing practice for those of Norse heritage. We will not go into physical shifting here but we are going to take the first steps towards that ability. Whether you want to develop it to the point of physical shifting or not is a personal matter, but you need to fully master shifting of the Spirit (Óðr). The other types are entirely optional and non-essential for rune mastery.

Before starting this practice, pick an everyday object from your environment. It can be a table, a chair or anything similar. The next step is, of course, shifting into the Spirit (Óðr). Once you have done so, focus on feeling the Spirit (Óðr). This is simply done by sensing it from head to foot as it is held within the energy body (Hamr). Having established a firm sense of it and its shape, proceed to will its shape to shift. What you want to shift into is the shape and look of whatever object you picked. For instance, if you selected a table or chair, your new Spirit (Óðr) shape MUST match that table or chair in every possible detail. There must be no differences whatsoever. Pay close attention to establishing as precise a shape as possible, copying your selected item. Now meditate on the fact that since your Spirit (Óðr) is now in the shape of that item, YOU are now that item.

Whilst doing this meditation, you need to feel yourself being the object completely. You need to lose all awareness of your body and only be aware of being the object you are working on. Eventually, you will shift into being that item. In effect, you will have transferred your awareness into that of the object you chose. It is important not to physically try to imitate the object. Instead you are shifting the shape of the Spirit (Óðr) and, by virtue of the mental reality laws where there is no space, your awareness automatically shifts into the correct position. There is no need to focus, intend or will this shift as it is totally automatic due to the laws functioning at the mental level of reality (in this case, like attracts like).

Once you have managed to accomplish this, feel the concept of the item, know it from being it, experience it, its purpose, its awareness (which is your awareness merged with it) and its essence. Your perceptions have to be and only be those of the object, nothing more, nothing less.

When you are ready to end this perception, simply shift your Spirit (Óðr) shape back to the shape of your own body. This will reverse the flow and you should feel yourself back in the Spirit (Óðr) which is in the energy body (Hamr) and in the physical body (Lik) of your usual happy self!

Quick Steps

1. Select an object you see on a daily basis.
2. Shift into the Spirit (Óðr) as outlined in the previous exercises.
3. Establish a good sense of the Spirit (Óðr).

Feel how it conforms to the shape of your body (Lik) but extends slightly beyond it.

4. Work from the feeling you have of your Spirit (Óðr) and will it to change, and reshape the confines of the shape the Spirit (Óðr) is conforming to.
5. Reflect on your new shape. What are its perceptions? What is it like to be in that new shape? What is the purpose the object you are now? How does your conscious mind function in that limited form? How is your awareness affected? What does it feel like?
6. Settle into your new perception.
7. You ARE whatever you shaped into. It is the entire extent of your perceptions and awareness at that particular point in time.
8. Having experienced as much of it as you want, gradually allow your Spirit (Óðr) to re-shape back to the form of your physical body (Lik).
9. Reaffirm your sense of the physical (Lik) and your Spirit (Óðr) flowing through the energy body (Hamr).

Developing this skill of Spirit (Óðr) shaping (shifting awareness) is very important and will be used extensively later on. It will also enable you to gain insight into how other things and even other people perceive. It also gives you an imprint of the awareness of everything you shift into and will change your thought patterns to new ones. Each shape has its own unique individual thinking and consciousness capabilities, and as you adopt a given shape, you will be subject to its thinking capabilities and patterns.

Óðr Shaping Into Runes
Becoming the Rune Flow

Having developed basic skills when it comes to shaping the Spirit (Óðr), it is time to take the next step and dive deep into the runic side of this practice. It is not really difficult by any stretch of the imagination – it just requires a little patience. What you will be doing is following exactly the same process as outlined in Shaping the Spirit (Óðr) with one major exception: the shape. Rather than choosing a random shape, we are going to be shaping our Spirit (Óðr) in the actual shapes of the runes themselves. This will achieve a deep and significant synergy in between yourself and the actual runic current for that specific rune. This is the fundamental step to both activation of the rune energy within yourself AND pulling the universal manifestations of that rune-stream into yourself.

One thing to be cautious about here. There are rune forces you will be very comfortable with, there are those you will be indifferent to AND there are those you will be naturally in opposition to. As you practice this, you will be pulling in all these runic powers and those you are in conflict with will try to run amok. The impact of introducing such a runic force into yourself will be to insert a disruptive element into your very Spirit (Óðr). Unfortunately, there is no short-cut here and you will have to work at it bit by bit until that runic energy becomes neutral and is no longer disruptive. Since this is occurring on the mental, intellectual, memory-based and perceptual side of things, you will be able to notice them very rapidly. Disruptive rune forces should not be worked on too much – only spend about 1/3 of the time on them that you would with any other. This introduces these disruptive influences gradually and makes them more manageable. If at any point they become unmanageable, simply use the ᛈ Vin (Wunjo) or ᛉ Ýr (Elhaz) runes to harmonise yourself and ensure you visualise those energies fading away from within yourself.

The practice is simple: select a rune to work with. Follow the Spirit (Óðr)-shaping practice stages given above and shape your Spirit (Óðr) to match a three-dimensional version of the rune. At that point, all you need to do is to mediate and will yourself to become the rune. As long as you are in trance from that point onwards, you ARE the rune, nothing more, nothing less, nothing else. For this stage of practice, unless you already have energetic references for the runes, use the colour deep red and let the rune's information flow through your awareness and sensory perception, informing you of what its nature actually is. You should avoid focussing on known rune characteristics and influences as they will only muddy the waters, so to speak. They refer to the application of runic energies to specific situations on very specific levels of reality and that is not what we are looking for here. At this point, what we want is for the entire runic current to flow through us, for our Self to recognise it and for that universal current to recognise our Self.

Quick Steps

1. Select a rune to work with (see outlines below).
2. Shift into the Spirit (Óðr) as outlined in the previous exercises.
3. Establish a good sense of the Spirit (Óðr), feeling how it conforms to the shape of your body but extends slightly beyond it.
4. Work from the feeling you have of your Spirit (Óðr) and will it to change and reshape to the confines of shape of the selected rune.
5. Allow your conscious awareness to sink into all that the rune is, all that it represents and all the possibilities it offers. For that brief period in time, YOU ARE THE RUNE.
6. Feel the rune's power and its currents flowing through you.
7. Settle into your new perceptions.
8. Having experienced as much of it as you want, gradually allow your Spirit (Óðr) to re-shape back to the form of your physical body (Lik).
9. Reaffirm your sense of the physical body (Lik) and your Spirit (Óðr) flowing through the energy body (Hamr).

Men should start with the fire-based runes as follows: ᛈ Perð (Pertho) – ᚠ Fé (Fehu) – ᚦ Þurs (Thurisaz) – ᚲ Kaun (Kenaz) – ᚾ Nauð (Nauthiz) – ᛦ

- Roadmap to High Galdr Runes -

Ýr (Elhaz) - ᛋ Sól (Sowilo) - ᛘ Dagur (Dagaz), then ᚠ Óss (Ansuz) - ᚱ Reið (Raidho) - ᚷ Gjöf (Gebo) - ᛏ Týr (Tiwaz) - ᛖ Maður (Mannaz) - ᚢ Úr (Uruz) - ᛃ Ár (Jera) - ᛒ Bjarkan (Berkano) - ᛖ Eykur (Ehwaz) - ᛜ Ing (Ingwaz) - ᛟ Óðal (Othala) - ᛁ Íss (Isa) - ᚺ Hagall (Hagalaz) - ᚹ Vin (Wunjo) - ᛚ Lögur (Laguz) - ᛇ Jór (Eihwaz)

ᚴᚠᚦᚲᚢᛏᛦᛋᛘᚨᚱᚷᛏᛖᚢᛊᛒᛗᛜᛟᛁᚺᚹᛚᛇ

Women should start with the ice-based runes as follows: ᛈ Perð (Pertho) - ᛁ Íss (Isa) - ᚺ Hagall (Hagalaz) - ᚹ Vin (Wunjo) then ᚠ Óss (Ansuz) - ᚱ Reið (Raidho) - ᚷ Gjöf (Gebo) - ᛏ Týr (Tiwaz) - ᛖ Maður (Mannaz) - ᚠ Fé (Fehu) - ᚦ Þurs (Thurisaz) - ᚲ Kaun (Kenaz) - ᛏ Nauð (Nauthiz) - ᛦ Ýr (Elhaz) - ᛋ Sól (Sowilo) - ᛘ Dagur (Dagaz) - ᛚ Lögur (Laguz) - ᚢ Úr (Uruz) - ᛃ Ár (Jera) - ᛒ Bjarkan (Berkano) - ᛖ Eykur (Ehwaz) - ᛜ Ing (Ingwaz) - ᛟ Óðal (Othala) - ᛇ Jór (Eihwaz)

ᚴᛁᚺᚹᚠᚱᚷᛏᛖᚠᚦᚲᚢᛏᛦᛋᛘᛚᚢᛊᛒᛗᛜᛟᛇ

There is no need to rush through things here, wasting time and effort either now or in future work which builds on this. Remember, revisiting these exercises often is highly recommended!

Communication and Use of the Hugr Raven

Before we can send the Twin Ravens of the mind to flight, the ability to communicate with them is essential – otherwise you will be attaining absolutely no benefit whatsoever. There are essentially three different ways to communicate with the Hugr Raven (the Minni Raven is a little different). No matter which method is used, remember to always start with events you can validate easily. In other words, send the Hugr Raven off to observe something you can then check. This is essential when developing the skills to communicate with it. Our minds are used to waddling in illusions, wishful thinking, misinterpretations and so forth. All of these need to be cut through so that you can perceive actual reality. The only way to do so for us is via observations on the physical level of reality first! Once you have perfect accuracy on perception and interpretation, you can move onto the energetic reality and then into higher ones. If these initial steps, no matter how long they take, are not followed, your ability to perceive will be riddled with inaccuracies. Not only that, but when you start dealing with the non-physical, which is far more fluid matter and energy, those inaccuracies will be exponentially increased. Not a good state of affairs, to say the least. Spend time to get this done right and the efforts will be paid back in more ways than you can imagine.

Since we are working within the Norse tradition, we are going to use the Raven when shaping the Hugr. It will be black with an outline or shimmering of your own energy hues. If you cannot perceive your own energies, it is a good idea to use a dark but vivid blue for the mind (Hugr) and a glowing grass green for the Minni. Those are their universal hues and once you start seeing energy and gain perceptions of your own, you can switch without even the slightest disruption. Once you have set the energy colour or feel for your Hugr, proceed to the exercise outlined below.

Setting the Hugr Raven to Flight

In order to awaken conscious control of the Hugr Raven, you will need to go into a slight trance. Simply sit with legs comfortable and hands on the respective leg. Do not cross the legs or the hands. Sitting in a chair with back support and legs down is the best for energy flow.

Relax, let go of all the tension, take a few breaths if needed and focus on relaxing (we really do not do this often enough, these days!). Let go of all the worries, fears, to do lists and so forth. Simply allow the world to fade from your awareness for the next 20 minutes; it need not even exist to your perceptions since it is not relevant.

Focus on your thoughts. Simply observe them whilst your mind stills. Ignore the thoughts which pop into your mind. As you do, you will notice that they do so less often. There is more time in between each thought which comes to mind. This is a sign of mild trance. The next step involves focusing on the cortex part of your brain. Simply think inside the forehead region. Once you get a feel for it, you should notice a mild pressure there. Then do exactly the same but on the whole of the left brain. Wait until the pressure surfaces here too.

The next step is a little tricky and, due to the nature of the practice, men will find it somewhat easier. The ladies just need to work a bit more at it – there is nothing stopping them getting the hang of it; it just needs a little more concentration and maybe a bit more patience. What you need to do is to shift your point of awareness into those two parts of the brain where the pressure has been felt, namely the left side and the inside of the front of the head (this is actually the back of the brain itself). As you concentrate, will yourself to be those parts of the brain. See yourself as them and only them. Your shape is their shape. That is the entirety of your being at this moment in time. Settle into that feeling. What does your brain feel like? What do the electrical impulses of the firing neurons in there feel like? What does the flow of electricity within it feel like? Lose yourself in being your brain. Will yourself to be in perfect harmony with it. After all, each and every cell in it is a part of you.

What this does is to increase both blood flow and the electrochemical activity within those regions of the brain. The ladies will sense a bilateral activation in the right side of the brain and the men will be more aware of such activation at the back of the head – the hindbrain (cerebellum). Just ignore those. Now from within the regions of the brain which are your current body or shape, will them to reshape into the form of a Raven. Feel it expanding outwards and backwards, see the focal point of vision tunnel out in front of you and FEEL the feathered wings. The claws will surface out of the core of the brain (deep inside).

Spend a few moments feeling and seeing yourself from within the Raven and adopting its perspective. Will the mind and reason to flow through it and will your conscious awareness to do so as well. This is a part of the Self which CAN carry consciousness (unlike the Hamingja). Feel yourself in total harmony with the Raven. You are the Raven, the Hugr. The ladies will find this step much easier due to having more mirror neurons than the chaps. Here, the gents will need to work a bit

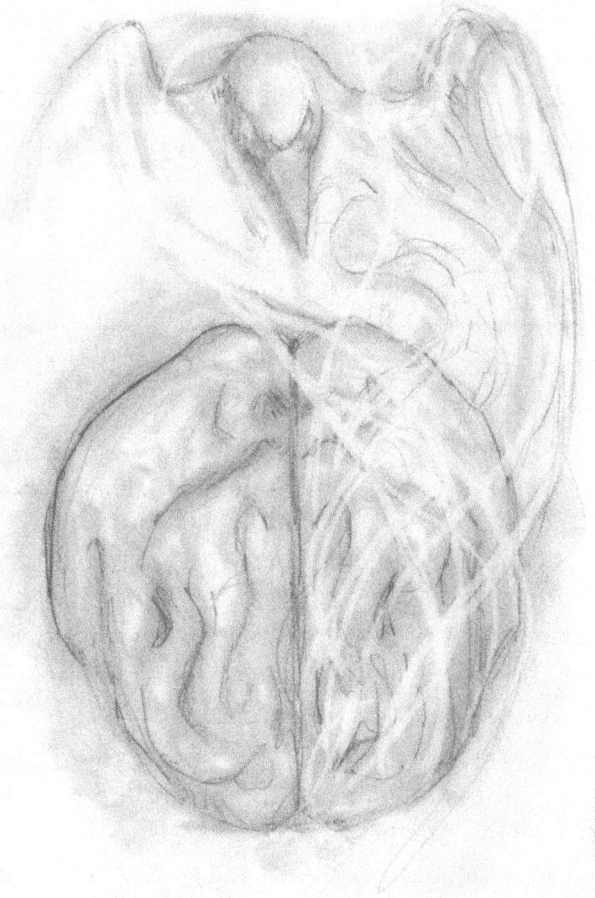

Hugr Raven rising out of
left side of the brain

harder on this step. A good focus is to feel the space around you as you are the Raven. This spatial awareness trick is your brain's speciality, gents! If you feel the Raven and the space you occupy as a Raven, then you should get a good response.

Take flight by simply willing yourself (or, if you have mastered intent, by intending yourself) to float above your head. Observe the room you are sitting in from that perspective. Record all you see.

After a few minutes, lower yourself and turn around moving outwards a little. In effect, what you want to achieve is this: from your Raven point of view, you should be floating with your Raven eyes staring right at the centre of your physical body's forehead. If it helps, focus on the bridge of the nose above the eyes. When ready, will yourself forward, entering the skull and re-merging with the brain part behind your forehead. Merge the Raven's shape back into the brain and will those things you have observed to flow back into your 'mind'.

A good tip here is to see the Raven as becoming less substantial and more akin to an energy shape which then spills into the brain. Resettle, allowing your perspective to shift back to your human eyes and perceptions. Then, simply expand your awareness all over your body. Remember to feel what it feels like; become aware of its form and the space it occupies. Slowly become aware of your environment and slip back out of the mild trance.

Once out of trance, the first thing to do is to look at your immediate environment and compare what you recall from looking through the Hugr Raven's eyes compared to what you see now. Make sure that all you have perceived from the Hugr Raven matches what you perceive with your eyes open. There might be things in different positions, missing items from tables, items which were imagined which are not actually there and so forth. Take note of how many discrepancies there are.

Quick Steps

1. Relax and allow the world to fade out of focus.
2. Ignore your thoughts. Just observe them flow into and out of your mind without engaging with them.
3. See how they eventually slow down in speed, until the amount of time between each new thought coming in and leaving your mind increases.
4. Focus in on the forehead brain region. Feel it and sense the build-up of mild pressure there.
5. Expand this sense to the left side of the brain.
6. Visualise yourself inside those parts of the brain to the exclusion of all else, until you are sensing and seeing things from the point of view of being inside those two parts of your brain.
7. Having gained a sense of being inside these brain regions, will yourself to reshape to the same shape as those parts of the brain. Here, you are using the shaping of the Spirit (Óðr) practice to become your own brain and only that.
8. Reflect on what it feels like to be your own brain. Feel the electric currents passing

through it, and the harmony of the waves upon waves of activity taking place there.

9. As soon as you have a solid perceptive footing, start reshaping to the form of a Raven but do so from the brain you are in right now. Just intend your Spirit (Óðr) to reshape and feel the stretching out of wings, the feathers forming, the head and beak elongating outwards and the claws forming from the lower parts of the brain.

10. As the form of the Raven emerges, allow all your perceptions to flow from the perspective of the Raven.

11. Spend some time feeling and sensing yourself in your new form. Get used to it, know it, feel it, be it. Then simply will your mind and reasoning capabilities to flow through it and within it.

12. Next feel the space around you (the Raven).

13. Spread your wings and take flight. Remember to keep your perspective LOCKED within the Raven, see your body under it as you are floating above it. Because the Raven is host of mind and reason, you can move within it as you do in your body (Lik) OR you can move as you would in your energy body (Hamr) – either option works. For now, if you do not know what this is all about, just move as you would in the physical body of a Raven.

14. Float around where your body is seated and observe around it. Take note of all you see.

15. When done, reverse the process. Typically, you can either land on the head and sink back into the brain, then reshape to it. You

can also turn around and, from within the Raven, point its beak straight to the midpoint in between your body's eyes and simply push into the head that way, then reshape to the brain shape. Either way works; pick whichever works best for you.

16   All that remains to be done is to reshape from the brain back into the shape of your physical body (Lik). Spend a few moments reaffirming your sense of the full body and how it feels, as well as how you feel within it.
17   Proceed to open your eyes and take a deep breath.
18   Not done yet! As soon as your eyes are open and you are back to normal perception mode, look around and compare all you saw as the Hugr Raven and all you see now. Note any inaccuracies in detail and note those observed things which match perfectly. Focus on the matches and tell yourself 'well done' or 'this is it' or something else along those lines. MAKE SURE YOU DO THIS AFTER EACH PRACTICE.

Next time you do this practice, repeat it all in exactly the same fashion, and once again, take note of any discrepancies. You will see that the more you practice this, the easier it will become to do all the shifts of perception AND the fewer and fewer discrepancies will be found.

This is extremely, EXTREMELY important. What you are doing is teaching your brain, your mind and your awareness to cut through illusions, wishful thinking and imaginings and to instead only take note of actual reality. It is an absolutely essential lesson for several parts of your Self to learn. If they fail to do so, your development will be plagued by illusory nonsense and ego-boosting wishful thinking, and will expose you to the vulnerability of being manipulated. This ability to cut through illusions and see straight to what is real is so essential, it cannot be stressed sufficiently. Lack of perseverance in this type of training is one of the key reasons why the mental and spiritual teachings available these days are so littered with non-sense, incorrect interpretations of ancient concepts and just made up foolishness interpreted as actualities. Always double-check things!

Once this pattern is ingrained in the Self, it will automatically cut through the nonsense to give you perceptions based on reality, whether you are looking at this physical reality or any of the others.

ESSENTIAL PRACTICES FROM THE BLOOD OF LÓÐURR AWAKENS

Key Work From The Blood of Lóðurr Awakens

In this third section, we will be looking at two of the most important foundations to master (in terms of preparation for High Galdr): the biological awareness (from the physical body (Lik)) and the energy body (Hamr). We will not be dealing with the Shadow Self (Sal) here since it falls more within the scope of Seiðr rather than pure Galdr and is covered in far more detail in *The Blood of Lóðurr Awakens*.

Here, we will be looking at Lóðurr's gifts to mankind, those of mobility (fluidity) see 'Gifts of Lóðurr' p.9 and 'Norse View of the Creation of Man' p.13 in *The Blood of Lóðurr Awakens*.

I would strongly suggest, once you are done with this section, to think about picking up a full copy of *The Blood of Lóðurr Awakens* for a more in-depth study of the topics at hand. The three parts of the Self covered, the physical body (Lik), energy body (Hamr) and shadow (Sal) are a real treasure trove of skills and potentials for all the work you do and ever will do.

From these practices, I recommend you start working in parallel. It is more than possible, and even advantageous to do the biological awareness work AT THE SAME time as doing the energy body (Hamr), providing you do them both. This is simply because as you increase your connection with your biological awareness (via physical body(Lik)), it will boost the effects and ease with which you can reach and get a response from your energy body (Hamr). That body will in turn increase your ability to work with your biological awareness. The two sets of practices interrelate and enhance each other's results. Whatever you do, avoid at all costs skipping the one for the other. It ultimately does not matter in the end if you prefer to focus on your biological awareness and physical body (Lik) first, then proceed to the energy body (Hamr) work, or if you have decided to do both simultaneously, as long as you do not skip the one or the other. You need to put the same amount of effort into them both and avoid the tendency of rushing through the one you find least exciting in order to get on with the other. What you will be trying to achieve is to merge your conscious awareness with your biological awareness (which is what modern-day linguistics refers to as your 'subconscious' mind) and produce a uniform awareness which is superior to both. It is with that awareness that you will be unleashing your High Galdr. This in turn opens your path to both the energy body (Hamr) and the shadow (Sal).

Completing those practices gives you the fundamentals to unleashing your Galdr and finally start working with actual Intent. The only remaining practices will then be learning visualisation works and the correct way in which to visualise. Once you have worked through these, you will be ready to pick up actual High Galdr work.

Body Awareness
Biological Awareness

This expresses itself in one of two ways, depending on the individual: the inner child or the inner beast. These manifestations are set for life and cannot be changed; they depend entirely on you as an individual. The former can be wild as well, and the latter can be your greatest friend and protector. It is important to realise the type of biological awareness you have, to accept it and work with it. What you should avoid doing at ANY cost is trying to judge it or classify one as better than the other. This is being judgmental and imposing human social conditioning on something which is so fundamentally biological that it surpasses all such judgements.

The biological awareness connects to the conscious awareness through the nervous system. The physical body (Lik), being the great foundation and integrator, has not evolved into a dual-nervous system structure randomly – far from it. The central nervous system and the autonomic nervous systems are separate yet interconnected (and highly hierarchical) for a good reason. They represent the two different types of awareness, each with its own consciousness. The former we call conscious and the latter we call subconscious or unconscious – it is truly neither of those, but those concepts are good enough to guide your thinking to it. For some reason, it seems incredibly difficult for 'modern' people to conceive of another type of consciousness within them operating outside of their awareness or control. Baffling...

A quick note here. Before anyone tries to take these concepts and twist them, the beast and child modes of the biological awareness ARE NOT a result of race or gender or anything like this. Do NOT go assuming this to be the case. There is infinite variety, and that includes infinite combinations of those who function along the lines of the one or the other. It is most unwise to assume that the one is better than the other or vice versa.

In our highly primitive approach to dealing with the Self, especially the biological self, rather than allow its own awareness to surface and take control from time to time in order to experience and grow, mankind tends to go all judgmental and tries to override it, over and over again, until eventually at some point or other, control is lost and the child within goes on a rampage or the beast within goes berserk (hint! hint!) and great damage is done. It is far better to allow these inner impulses to be satisfied in an understanding and non-destructive manner under the supervision of the conscious mind. This cycle has been perpetuated for ages, and in the past it was given labels such as possession by 'evil', 'devils', 'demons' and so forth, whereas in fact it was nothing more than the biological awareness finally overwhelming the conscious controls and restrictions and going on a rampage, due to never being allowed to experience what it needs to grow. These days, we see it yet again in all these so-called mental disorders swarming the population. Mankind is being pushed to evolve and that means so is his or her biological awareness. Restrict it, and that very push – which it will feel and experience millions of times more directly and potently than our conscious mind – will cause it to go haywire. Remember, this biological awareness has DIRECT access to all systems in our bodies, including the chemical, biological, neural, genetic and so forth! It can do whatever it wills or feels it needs to short-circuit the Spirit (hence conscious awareness) in whatever way it finds best.

Why turn your own biology against yourself? It is here for us to experience growth and to evolve with us. Making it an enemy as mankind is doing *en masse* is the road to madness and failure.

Functions of Biological Awareness

You might be wondering what exactly the purpose of this biological awareness is, and why you need to bother with it. The answer is simple; it is the basis of our complete awareness. This might be a little confusing as a statement, so let us put it into more familiar terminology: you have consciousness, awareness, what people call 'subconscious' or 'unconscious' (basically that other mind which process sensory and information without our conscious mind's involvement), and what we call hyper-consciousness (when your consciousness functions at much higher levels of existence, such as when perceiving directly from energy (see *The Spirit of Húnir Awakens – Parts 1 & 2*). In human beings, all these modes of consciousness and awareness (and hence perception) are separate. We only have access to them whilst they are functional and even then, they might elude us completely. Because the basis of the human being is the physical (or condensed energy, if you prefer), that is our starting point. It is from where consciousness in all humans arises. Biological awareness is not only the link between the Spirit (Óðr) and physical body (Lik), but is the key to both the energy body (Hamr) and the shadow (Sal). By maturing and growing it, we also gain direct experience and perceptions of the entire energy level of reality (and Self). This in turn gives us full access to the all-elusive ability of our Self, which is 'intending'.

Taking this concept a step further, if you look at the whole Self and its nine-fold structure, you will see that the physical body (Lik) is a central point of it. By awakening our conscious harmonisation (and hence integrating) with our biological awareness, we expand our (conscious) awareness into the energy body (Hamr) and shadow (Sal) as well. This achieves a unification of the three parts of our Self at the energetic level, and links them directly with the Spirit (Óðr). Because the Spirit (Óðr) manifests as mind (Hugr) and memory (Minni), those are already integrated and within our conscious reach. Hence we now have the mental/spiritual level of the Self fully integrated with the energetic. Six parts of the Self work in union. In *The Breath of Oðin Awakens*, we saw how the breath (Önd) is made to flow through our DNA and blood, and that this pulled Megin-charged breath into the biological awareness. We learnt to expand the Hamingja throughout the physical body (Lik) which in turn introduced it to the biological awareness, and since the Fylgja (inherited/ancestral spirit) is bound to us at birth, that flows through it as well, via the DNA. As you can see, those latter three brought the archetypal parts of the Self into the flesh. Then we brought more and more of the mental level and now we finally awaken the flesh itself and bring in the energy body (Hamr) and shadow (Sal): this completely unifies ALL the parts of the Self and initiates its harmonisation. Full harmonisation takes time and persistence but the key 'introductions' are all made and these parts of the Self start to exchange information, energy, power, experiences and so forth. The result? A growth in the whole Self, a crossing over of all the levels of Creation within the Self. Slowly, step by step, you become more and more a central point in your own Creation. Your awareness expands and so does your influence (as well as your stability!).

This, ladies and gents, is why the Biological Awareness is such an important part of our Self. It is the foundation into which we ground ALL other parts of the Self and start their unification: we become WHOLE. It is only from this point of being that we can start to get to know our true Self, what and who we are. It is also from this point that we can start to influence life and creation. It is at this point that the Spark of Self can become a Flame of Self capable of radiating its own uniqueness throughout the ENTIRE Self and eventually into Creation itself.

The golden rule is to always give the body what it strives for, its own cellular intelligence also NEEDS to grow, just as our minds do. But wait sometimes the desires of the body cannot be fulfilled – for instance, when things it would want lead to breaking the laws of the land. Yes, that is correct: it is possible, due to the fact that we live in an overly legalistic and politically correct social system. In these cases, there is no point in getting into trouble; simply sending out an intent to the body fused with the reasons why (it is impossible to do without causing it even more harm, such as being in jail, for instance) will suffice. What typically happens in these cases is that after sufficient 'pressure' from such impossibilities of experience and the growth of the biological need for those experiences, the innate cellular biology will start to pull on other resources it has access to which by default, we do not, in order to satisfy those experiential needs. These primarily are the physiological energy systems, the energy body (Hamr) and the shadow body (Sal). It is directly linked to them – more so than our conscious awareness could ever be. As such, it can force them into active functioning in order to displace awareness to another realm of possibilities, in order to gain that experiential knowledge and energy it needs for growth. When the mind and body are in harmony, this type of bypassing of the human limited realms in Midgard can occur smoothly, as the cellular intelligence will know that our awareness can carry those experiences (well their knowledge/informative parts) via memory (Minni) back to it, and the energy body (Hamr) and/or shadow (Sal) can carry the energetic ones. This is why harmony of body and mind is so vitally important. **The mind stirs the physicality into a new range of possibilities and that physically forces the mind to experience them.** Ultimately, it benefits both mind and body; each one grows, hence the Spirit and Flesh evolve in synchronicity.

If your biological awareness is told about the extraordinary and that it cannot access it, it will awaken the energy body (Hamr) or Shadow Self (Sal) to gain access. Once the energy body (Hamr) and shadow (Sal) have experienced them, those experiential energies are brought back to boost the cellular awareness.

Awakening the Bodily Awareness & Intelligence

Awakening might be a somewhat misleading term to use, since the body is always awake – or you would be not only dead, but decomposed. What we are instead achieving is a type of awakening of conscious awareness to the biological one. We are seeking to bring the two closer together and allow your conscious mind to communicate and connect with the body. In order to do so, they need to know each other!

To get started, you will first have to master the 'Shaping the Óðr' practice.[23] It is essential in many practices. If you have not, you should do so. Without it, you will not be able to proceed much further.

What you are going to be doing is reshaping your Spirit (Óðr) into the shape of every organ of your body as follows:

Lungs
Anus
Right eye
Left eye

Stomach
Right ear
Left ear
Whole spine
Left hand
Right hand
Right arm
Left arm
Left leg
Right leg
Left kidney
Right kidney
Diaphragm
Spleen
Abdomen
Liver
Throat
Testicles/ovaries
Right side of nose
Left side of nose
Gallbladder
Brain
Pancreas
Whole gut (Colon + small intestine + appendix)
Heart
Bladder
Urethra
Women: ovaries (inside the lower abdomen, one on the left, the other on the right)
Men: Penis and testicles
Women: Vagina
Women: Clitoris
Women: Womb (VERY IMPORTANT)
Men: Prostate gland (found just above the inside of the anus and midpoint up the urethra)
Adrenal glands (found at the top of each kidney)
Thyroid gland (gland in two parts in front of the windpipe)
Hypothalamus (just above the pituitary gland and optic chiasm, also straight behind the nose)
Thymus

In working the brain, you will start with the whole brain, then do the same with the following subdivisions:

Left side of brain only
Right side of the brain only
Frontal cortex only
Corpus colostrum (the thick nerve strip running from the top view of the brain from left to right)
Cerebellum (small brain at the back of head)
Pineal gland (mid-cranium, straight behind nose)
Pituitary gland (base of the brain)
Brain stem (where spine and brain connect)

Then you will reshape into the following:

Skeleton/bones
Spine
Nervous system (autonomous – body nervous system, not brain)
Brain nervous system

If you are unsure where a given organ is in your body, time to go and look it up. There is ample literature available and quite a few good references with detailed imagery online to refer to.

With the reshaping into nervous systems, you will just need to follow your bodily awareness and intuition because there are countless subtle variations in how individual nerves flow, connect and wrap in each and every one of us. It is impossible to capture them all in illustrations. By the time you reach working with the nervous system, the biological awareness will be aware of what you are doing and assist you.

Having done all of these, you will then proceed to do the same with the muscles in your body, and finally the skin (do not neglect the skin!).

With each of these reshapings, the process is exactly the same in terms of steps:

1. You reshape the Spirit (Óðr) to match the organ/body system.
2. You intend to be it. You feel yourself as it.
3. You then try to perceive its immediate environment. For instance, if you are the liver during your practice, what is happening around the liver on the outside? What fluids are coming into it? What is it sending out? How is it responding and to what is it responding? And so forth. This is a sensory practice where you feel/sense, NOT an intellectual one.
4. Your meditation has to be so deep that you become the liver. You have its shape and you are gaining insight into its purpose and functions. Do not try to interfere with ANY of them. Instead, just observe and experience; query them.
5. Once you have achieved a good union with the liver, intend to be at one with it.
6. Feel it, feel what it is like to be the liver, totally unify with it.
7. Bask in that unity.
8. Then reflect on how it is doing all that it needs to do. Intend to connect with the millions upon millions of liver cells. Acknowledge them, feel them, observe just how much intelligence each and every one of them holds on its own and how they all hold together as 'the liver'.
9. Next, intend yourself (as conscious awareness now united with the liver), to merge with that of the liver cells individually and as a whole. You are becoming part of them and they of you.

Take this step slowly and be thorough with it.

10 Just before you are about to end, it is optional, but definitely worth doing, to send out a sensation of 'thank you' or a sense of gratitude. It is after all thanks to each of the cells and organs as a whole that you are alive and thinking and doing!

11 When you are ready to end, simply reshape the Spirit (Óðr) back into that of your entire body and refocus on becoming at one with the whole body (Lik).

12 You need to feel each organ and unite with it exactly as it is.

Some people will have undergone various surgeries and some might even not have a 'whole' organ or it might be diseased. With these practices, you will notice a gap in the biological awareness and quite often a sense of blame from that awareness directed at you. This is something you are going to have work through. It is impossible to fill the gaps but it is possible to fix the sense of friction or blame an organ's awareness can have with your conscious mind. It is natural it will blame you. If you were born with a health issue or gained it during your youth or as a result of environmental factors, you will not sense any blame but more of a call for help. Remember, you are responsible for it. Communicate with it. As soon as you have completed one organ/system, move onto the next until you complete them all.

When you are communicating with it, it is important to avoid using words. They have absolutely no meaning to your biology. Use sensing and feeling, or pure thought (see *The Spirit of Húnir Awakens – Part 2*), or even better, use both. Remember, here we are, not looking at healing anything, simply we are connecting with and learning about all the parts of our own inner universe at the physical manifestation of the energetic level of our Self.

These practices serve a twofold purpose: the first is connecting with the biological awareness one step at a time and the second is gaining skill in projection of awareness. It is much easier to project and maintain that new locale within your Self than it is without – hence we always start by dealing with the inner physical, which is the most familiar, then move onto the inner pure energetic and finally step out to the outer.

Having done all of these, the final steps involve reshaping into the:

> Cerebrospinal fluid (found flowing throughout the spine up into the brain)
> The lymph system
> The blood system (master this one well; it will be used extensively in the 'Blood – Crystallised Megin and Life Essence' see *The Blood of Lóðurr Awakens* p.103).
> The respiratory system

With these, what you do is reshape yourself into the system itself through which these substances flow. Let us take the blood, for example. Here, you take on the shape of veins and arteries, and feel the flow of blood through them as outlined in the practice above. The second step involves spilling your Spirit (Óðr) into the blood itself. In this shaping, you are the blood flowing through the system you just experienced being in the previous step. Note: here we are not shaping into the heart; that was done in the organ reshaping. Instead, you are reshaping into the arteries used by the heart and feeling the blood pumping through you.

Last but most certainly not least, and probably one of the most important parts of this practice, you will need to reshape into the spaces in between, within your physiology. This is a tricky one to do but the greatest effort should be made to master it. Here we are talking about the spaces in between nerves, the spaces in between bones, the spaces in between cells, the pores in your skin where the spaces between skin cells are found and so forth. Getting this right takes time and requires a relatively solid biological awareness working with you. Whatever you do, do not skip this. It is an essential prerequisite for the work you will be doing with your Shadow Self (Sal). Unless this is done, there is no work possible with the Shadow Self (Sal).

Doing these serves as a precursor to building or rather shaping the energy body (Hamr) which is very much misunderstood. It is typically thought of as the blueprint for the physical – in fact, it is a blueprint but not only for the physical, which also has the DNA and epigenetics as well as environmental factors to shape it. The energy body (Hamr) is the blueprint built from the physical, which ultimately evolves into becoming the blueprint for the entire Self. We will look at this in more detail in a later section.

- ROADMAP TO HIGH GALDR RUNE WORK -

Body Shapes and Energy Types

We have seen how to make use of biological awareness, or at least how to master our first few steps in that direction. When dealing with the physical body (Lik) in our physical reality, it is necessary to bring the two into focus, otherwise all the things we do on a daily basis will have a significant impact without you being even aware of it. Most notably, we are going to look at how things we commonly interact with affect it: food, exercise, stress and so forth. Naturally, it is impossible to look at each and every one in complete detail – that would be impractical – but enough information can be given to guide you in the proper direction.

Body Types

Many people try and pursue a healthier lifestyle for the sake of well-being and longevity. Others do not care much about it at all and seek to enjoy life as much as they possibly can, irrespective of what may happen down the line. Each to his or her own. However, a rune mystic cannot afford such a luxury (nor can anyone else seeking to work with energy or what could be loosely called that beyond the usual daily work, friends, shopping, TV and gossiping cyclic routine human beings enjoy so much).

For us, health is absolutely paramount due to the fact that any physiological impairment we might have will reduce our energy perception and use abilities, and will cause the Megin to flow in order to heal/maintain the body. It will also weaken our general energy reserves which are already extremely minimal, as is the case for any human Being, irrespective of health status quo. When the physical body (Lik) is in distress, this further disrupts the inner balance and harmony we need, and then our biology sees our minds and Self as an opponent against which it needs to work. This leads to all sorts of additional complications which wreck our entire energy system. Such problems then cause the energy body (Hamr) and shadow Self (Sal) to be immensely weakened. Remember, they gain energy from the excess the physical accumulates! It also makes concentration difficult and keeps the mind hindered from achieving the silencing needed for so much. With all these parts of Self out of order (literally), there is no power for intending. This effectively removes the key to achieving anything with energy, no matter how powerful or knowledgeable you might have become. Naturally, once you have moved beyond the limitation of the physical being your only foundation, and you have an active biological awareness in your energy body and/or shadow Self, when the physical weakens, it does not disrupt things to such a degree (if at all). But in order to get to that stage, you need as perfect health as possible.

We have looked at how our physiological organs have specific energy functions. These will not be able to function if the physical body (Lik) is making use of the energy to repair or work around a defect of some sort. If you have a long-term condition, the only way to counter it is to increase the amount of energy you take in to make up for the loss. The more conditions and the greater their physiological impact, the greater that energy will have to be. Very long-term conditions usually rewire the body to some extent and the energy body (Hamr) to a greater one. This means you might have to manually rewire part of the energy systems in order to re-establish proper 'wiring' and stop the harmful or debilitating ones.

Body Shapes as Energy Indicators

Many people love the saying of you having to look inside for your Self. In fact, this is totally wrong. The inner reflects the outer and the outer in turn reflects the inner. Our physical bodies (Lik) are the central core of our energy body (Hamr) which in turn is a central point of our Spirits (Óðr). When you are looking at someone's physical body (Lik), you are looking at one of the innermost parts of them.

The physical shapes we have are a direct reflection of the state of our health and our energy types as well as energy flows. They are also excellent indicators of how structured the energy body (Hamr) and shadows (Sal) are. Inversely speaking, the stronger the energy body (Hamr) and shadow self (Sal), the better it will result in changes to the physical body (Lik)'s shape.

General rules: the more curvature in your shape, the more complex your energy structures and the greater their scope (diversity). For instance, if you look at muscular man, you will see a massive amount of curvature, where each muscle is shaped in its own distinct way, each one having a curving of physical shape. Compare that to someone who is super slim: this man would have only the most basic shapes making up his limbs and body, while everything else is pretty much straight in comparison. Such an individual would have very simplistic energy systems with far less diversity in energy type than the former.

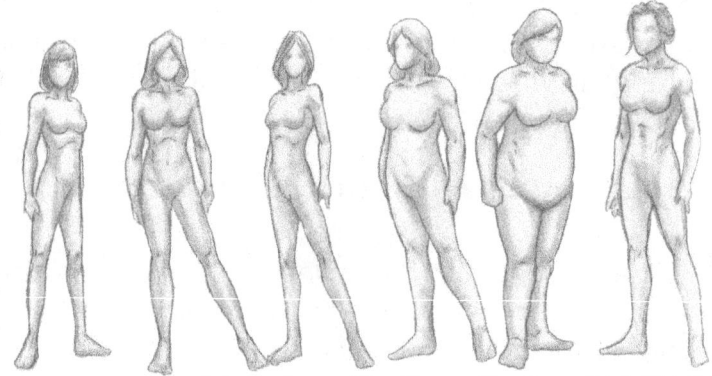

Female body shapes: Slim, Fit, very Slim, Curvy, Fat & Athletic

Fat stored in the body has the energetic effect of slowing it down and making it more sluggish. It is the same with substances such as oils, but there are no slippery effects, energetically speaking. The more fat you carry, the slower your overall vibration will be and the less likely will your energy be to merge with other energy. To be able to be transmitted, the more sluggish and slow its transmission, the less brilliance it will have. Remember, fat cells store surplus energy, toxins and things such as excess stress hormones. Reducing it does not only involve reducing your amount of food intake but also limiting exposure to chemicals, toxins and stress.

Muscle produces energy – both physical and pure energy – in great quantities, and it also speeds up the overall vibrational rates of energy as well as adding to the overall energetic gravity. Too much muscle will slow it down due to the vast increase in energetic gravity. Developing muscle is essential not only to overall health but also to the body's energy system, efficiency and quality.

Brighter skin, hair, nipple and eye tones emit and transfer energy, while darker tones absorb it. The extra melatonin causes this absorption in terms of physical light or energy such as sunlight. Those with thinner hair have highly vibrating spiritual energy. It is more ethereal, whereas those with thicker hair have a stable vibration

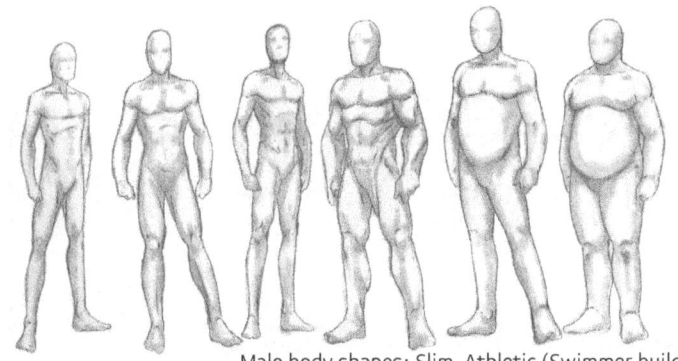

Male body shapes: Slim, Athletic (Swimmer build), very Slim, Atheltic (bodybuilder build), Fat, Obese

of energy and are spiritually more grounded – think more earthen. Hence those individuals with the former will have a propensity towards more abstract energy types, whereas those with the latter will be more in tune with nature, elemental and those types of spiritual energies in their environments.

All that is said for the energy in the above descriptions also applies to the energy in general as you have it flowing through you. For instance, if you are a muscular man and you use a runic vocalisation, it will flow much faster and have a much higher vibration than a man who is slim or fat. If you are very muscular, such as a bodybuilder, you will unleash a greater density of energy through your bodies (it will have more punch and greater concentration) but will vibrate at a lower level than would for a man with a muscular swimmer's build. That man would have a higher vibration but less density in his energy flow. Simple. An overweight man would have a very sluggish, low-vibration energy flow, which would move as if it was making its way through sludge and so forth. When men have energy flow, theirs is more fiery and dynamic, while women's is subtler, persistent and more 'together', with longer-term effects in comparison to men's 'more punch and power but only now' patterns.

Impact of Body Form – The Three Fundamental Forces

Having gained a solid understanding of form and its impact, it is time to have a look at how underlying forces give rise to specific forms in manifestation with respect to the human body. This influence comes from what we call the fundamental forces, which manifest our physiology. Each one of us has a specific foundational shape in our bodies. This shape is determined by our genetics, our Spirit (Óðr) and most importantly, our Spark of Self. It cannot be changed even when we adapt or push it towards another shape. No matter how much you want it to change, it will remain fundamentally set. You can make slight changes – you can, by violating the sanctity of the body, make substantial ones at that – but you cannot change the whole of the underlying shape itself. The more fit you are, the less fat you hold, the truer the expression of this fundamental force in your physicality will manifest. It is always odd how people persistently want to force change on their bodies rather than work with what they have. Perfecting your shape is the key, not violating it to make it more like another by violating body sanctity.

These three forces are very simple to understand in elemental terms (we will leave their runic expressions for the time being to avoid overcomplicating things):

Flowing Force: Think of this as a combination of air (or wind) and ice. It is cold, extremely mobile, rapid and flowing. It is delicate and all-pervasive, a balancing force which carries you upwards. Unlike the water type of force, this one is dry – think of air with no humidity. Due to its constantly flowing nature the rapid ability to change from state to state is perfectly expressed by it, as well as an irregular nature. Do not confuse this with being chaotic – it has order within itself but when observed its changing pattern means that it is impossible to fixate a definition of characteristics upon it. Simply, as soon as you try and pin its nature down, it will have changed and become something different.

The Solidifying Force: This force shares characteristics of elemental earth and sea. It has a strong sense of gravity within it, a solidity. It has weight, yet is both solid and soft. Because of its heavy gravity it is very steady, and once on a path it is extremely difficult to throw it off that path. However, unlike the flowing force, the solidifying force moves slowly. In terms of moisture, it has a lot, which almost makes it feel oily to the senses and the richness within it is very comforting and protective (think of it in terms of an overabundance of nutrition).

The Burning Force: This force can be thought

of as a mix of earthly and fire elemental forces. It is hot, dry and has incredible intensity. It is a very sharp and acidic force as well as extremely light. Because of this, it manifests a very penetrating approach to all things it makes contact with. With the earthly influences, rich acidic scents can be picked up when coming into contact with them.

Now that we have a basic view of these three forces, we can see how they dictate our physical body (Lik) shapes. Each body has one of these forces which dictates its shaping. Others can be introduced by willed practices, but even if you overload on any of the other two, all you will achieve is throwing yours out of balance, rather than changing the dominant force dictating your physical shape.

People with flowing force bodies have very fine, almost sculpted lines and curvature in their bodies. Their muscles have a very defined look and they tend not

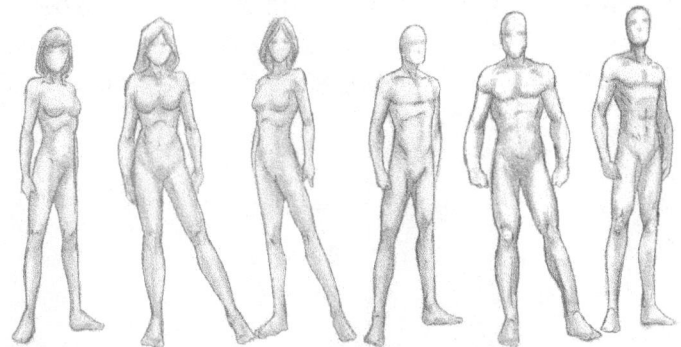

Flowing Force body shapes:
(Female) Standard flowing, Strong flowing, Weak flowing,
(Male) Standard flowing, Strong flowing and Weak flowing.

to hold onto much bloating, if any at all. Individuals with this force have thinner and lighter frames than their counterparts and are blessed with a high degree of agility. In terms of builds when perfected at the gym, these individuals will end up with what is often referred to as a 'swimmer's build' and no matter how hard they try, they will not be able to achieve the extremely bulky bodybuilder look. Energy in these individuals is overwhelming but also fades rapidly. It is best compared to a gush of wind which carries everything in its path away and is then gone. These individuals have dry skin, and run colder than their counterparts. In dreamwork, these lucky ladies and gents will have lighter sleep and a tendency towards fully functional consciousness during sleep. Their minds are always running at hyper-speed, thoughts stream faster than others and they often either end up speaking rapidly, or making incredible jumps in logic which makes it difficult for non-flowing types to follow. They are always on the lookout for new exciting challenges and hate being 'pinned down', even though it would do them a lot of good to be, from time to time.

Those with the solidifying force are practically the opposites of the flowing force individuals. These people have strong builds and a steady flow of constant physical energy. Their frames are larger and they can carry bulk

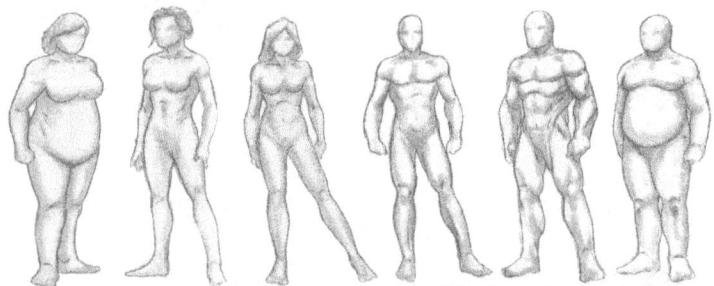

Solidifying Force body shapes:
(Female) Overweight solidifying, Strong solidifying, Standard solidifying
(Male) Standard solidifying, Strong solidifying and Overweight solidifying.

much easier than their counterparts. They have soft and smooth skin (thanks to the moisture in their physiological force) and very rich, thick hair. It is incredibly easy for them to put weight on. Their minds are far more settled and steadier than those of other types. These individuals have exchanged the ability to reach the heights of those of the flowing force, for the ability to maintain stability effortlessly. In effect, unlike the flowing force individuals, the solidifying ones will not rapidly shift from ecstasy to depression in a cyclic manner, but will maintain an overall balanced midpoint between those two extremes.

Individuals who are of the burning force body type are typically medium sized in body frame. They have excellent digestive systems, seem to have an endless

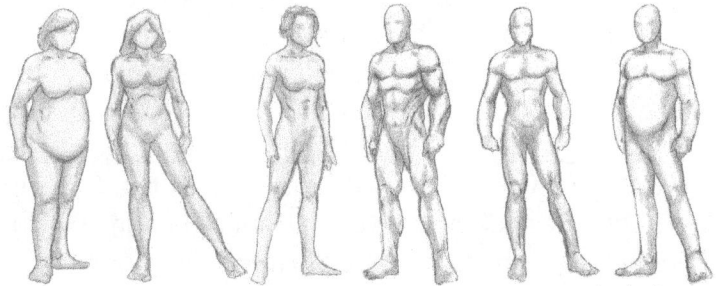

Burning Force body shapes:
(Female) Overweight burning, Athletic burning, Standard burning,
(Male) Athletic burning, Standard burning and Overweight burning

store of energy, high sex drives and can be very predisposed to hair loss. Their bodies are always warm and they adapt very rapidly to both hot and cold climates. Putting weight on is easy for these lucky ones but they have difficulty handling that additional weight. These individuals have a tendency to be either in great shape or fat – it is the one or the other. Their minds are very rapid in comparison to the solidifying individuals, but somewhat slower than the flowing ones. The burning force individuals are very direct and outspoken. They will tell you exactly what they think, whether you like it or not, unlike the reserved flowing force minds. These men and women are a hive of activity in their own right: constant challenges, constant new ventures, the more the better!

These basic forces, one of which gave rise to your shape, will dictate ALL the tendencies and manifestations of the Self. Remember, your physical body (Lik) shape dictates the shapes of practically all other parts of the Self. They will also dictate how your runic energies manifest. For instance, a ᚠ Fé (Fehu) fire rune for the burning types will be the most explosive energy you can get, the same rune for the flowing types will be the furthest reaching and quickest expansive manifestation of the fires and for the solidifying types, it will be the hottest and most tangible. They also dictate how strong one's work is on each of the three levels of reality, where the solidifying types will have the greatest advantages on the energetic levels (Lik, Hamr and Sal), the burning types will have the main advantage at the mental level (Óðr, Hugr, and Minni) and the flowing types on the archetypal (Önd, Hamingja and Fylgja). Needless to say, most "advantage" does not mean the other types cannot function on those levels – it will just be a little more of a challenge for them, that is all. We will be returning to these three forces at many other points in time. It is a good idea to get a basic grasp of them here.

A Few Words on Muscle

Muscle is an endocrine organ. It is also a substantial biological energy generator. Men here have a massive advantage in their ability to add muscular bulk. However, knowing how to use that bulk is key. All too often, these days we often see people in a state of being fat, overweight or so slim that they look like a skeleton wrapped in skin with a thin layer of flesh. Both these states are highly unhealthy, irrespective of what the mainstream and health movements are trying to promote. Let us look at the underlying reasons as to why this is the case (in energetic terms).

Human muscle is used by our bodies to produce force and motion by using energy. It is also an endocrine organ which controls the balance of catabolic and anabolic functions in the body. From an energetic point of view, muscle is essential for two key reasons: it produces energy and condenses it, but not only that, it is used to store it as well. When the muscle fibres contract (especially with skeletomuscular) they make the produced energy vibrate as well as releasing the stored energy. It literally causes a vibrational stream or wave to radiate out. The more muscle you have, the more powerful those vibrational waves, the more of them occur and the longer they last. The smooth muscle in our bodies causes the energies to flow with a gentler force along the path of their fibres. This is both a transformational function and a carrier one, where the explosive energies released by the skeletomuscular fibres are softened and made to flow through the soft muscle tissue. Needless to say, having as much muscle as possible will give you the most benefit in terms of energy. In addition, we will see at a later point in time how to use muscle to condense and make semi-physical runic energy. The average adult male has about 6% more muscle mass than the average adult woman[30] and due to their ability to build muscle, men can greatly increase their muscle mass, which they should do as a matter of utmost importance. **It is the MOST significant spiritual development step anyone can take.**

The main reason for us being in bodies of flesh and those forming the apex of the energetic level of the Self indicates just how important the physical body (Lik) actually is to our entire being. Most will think that cannot be right, surely? How can the body have such a profound impact and function? Unfortunately for everyone, it is, and it is a reality which is deeply mystical in its own right. We will go into this below. Since the mind (Hugr) and the energy body (Hamr) are not naturally directly connected, we struggle in reaching it and its perceptive mechanisms. More often than not, reaching the energy body (Hamr) requires substantial energy reserves which are free (not used by other physiological or mental processes). As discussed in *The Spirit of Húnir Awakens (Parts 1 & 2)* there is very scarce if any of this free energy in mankind, so amplifying the physiological sources and stores of energy is an essential step in increasing our total available energy.

A Few Words on The Nervous System

The nervous system is the main communication network for our physical body (Lik) and its energy systems. Very large portions of the scientific community are trying to study and learn as much about it as possible. There is much information and disinformation out there about its capabilities and functions. For our purpose, we will leave those specifics for another discussion and instead take a brief look at the energetic side of things. The spine and the nervous system flowing out of it are the anchor of your Self. They are also what one grounds into. When people talk about having to ground and all that nonsense, what they fail to realise is that the very fact that we are in physical bodies means we ARE grounded. If you need to reaffirm your foothold, all you do is focus on your spine, feel it and pull your energy into it. It is easy to do because that is the energetic function of the spine – just will or intend it and it will work. Energy flows through the nervous system – both physical energy and non-physical. Before engaging in too much energy and runic work, it is an excellent idea to find a proper chiropractor and make sure the spine is properly functioning and loosened with an adjustment or two. The difference it makes is very acute when trying to make energy flow through it.

    We will look at the spine and brain in a lot of detail at a later point in time. For the time being, it is worth keeping in mind that the nervous system is the communication network of your biological awareness. In other words, it is even more important than you could have suspected.

- Roadmap to High Galdr Rune Work -

Energy Body (Hamr) Fundamentals

Many different cultures share many different views on what we have come to call, in our modern area, the 'energy body' – also referred to in a more traditional context as the human soul. Because of the 'globalistic' nature of knowledge sharing, this has more often than not resulted in a mish-mash and horrible blending of what one can term the spaghetti-understanding of the topic. In addition, we have the problem of variations in the fundamental structures of the energy body (Hamr) dependent on gender, race, ancestral heritage and so forth. The overriding conception of the energy body (Hamr) being just that – a body of energy resulting in the assumption that this structure of the Self will always be alike for everyone – is a critical misconception. Existence values individualisation and the entire evolutionary drive is to produce as many unique and individual life forms as possible. As a matter of energetic fact, if two or more energy bodies (Hamur) were the same, they would fuse into a single one. The more alike one is to the other, the more their boundaries merge, according to the law of *like attracting like*.

This unfortunately means that in order to gain an in-depth knowledge of your energy body (Hamr) and its underlying capabilities, you will need to go and search through the original teachings of whichever racial background you come from and look at what those teachings provide, in terms of specific information with regard to your energetic heritage. A quick note on gender: the energy body (Hamr) will always match the natural biological gender which you have been born. Unfortunately, there is no surgery or treatment available to change that, other than creating a new energy body (Hamr) and replacing the existent one. As you can imagine, a feat still well beyond the capabilities of most.

As far as inherited characteristics, you can easily discover those from various stories your parents and grandparents tell you about various members of your family. These are critically important in discovering how your ancestors have shaped future generations' energy bodies (souls or Hamur).

Because it is impossible to enter into all these details, some of which are so personal that it would be impossible to put in a book, we will look at the generic characteristics of an energy body instead. The trick to apply when delving into the more specific areas is to remember that the runes were inscribed upon ALL things (and also life forms) in creation. It matters not what gender, race or ancestry you come from, as they will all be there (with the exception of ᛟ Óðal (Othala)). The Jarls have an additional set of three runes in their energy bodies, but since we are not going to look at those, all the information in here applies to everyone!

The Cycle of Existence of The Hamr

When you ask most, defining the energy body (or even the soul) seems to be very problematic. Everyone seems to have some form of unconscious grasp of it, but when it comes into the realm of mind and logic (Hugr), almost everyone struggles to pinpoint its nature or function. This is not surprising, purely due to the fact that as far as the complete structure of the Self is concerned the mind/intellect (Hugr) is not directly connected to the energy body (Hamr) – it has to go through the Spirit (Óðr) which is connected to the physical body (Lik), and then through the body (Lik) (via biological awareness) to the energy body (Hamr). In other words, it traverses a type of maze through the structures of the Self to even get to the energy body (Hamr), let alone start to analyse and learn about it. Additionally, the second point of difficulty arises from the fact that the Hamr is a body of energy and understands (or interacts) with things in terms of pure energy, it is a 'fluid' body. Hence, when dealing with it, there is a complete total lack of terms of interpretation and understand which our minds need to in order to learn about it. However, having worked through *The Spirit of Húnir Awakens (Parts 1 & 2)* and through the biological awareness practices (and hopefully the Hamingja ones too in *The Breath of Oðin Awakens*), your mind should be able to start interacting with this level of reality without having to have recourse to logic or be limited by linguistics. Always leave the interpretation of your experiences until AFTER the entire experience has been experienced! And be aware that your interpretation and understanding of these will change as your scope of conscious awareness grows. As discussed above, we also have the problem of people assuming the energy system of the physical body (Lik) as being the energy body (Hamr) itself to contend with.

Perceiving the Energy Body (Hamr)

It is important to practice sensing your energy body (Hamr) before trying to work with it. This sensing will allow you to expand your biological awareness further into and throughout the energy body (Hamr). It also prepares the energy body (Hamr) for future blending with the other parts of the Self, which is essential in mastering and knowing the Self!

Start by siting with your hands on your legs (quads). Sit perfectly still and just breathe, relax and still your mind. Let the tension fade away whilst keeping your thoughts from rambling on. Instead, focus on how your body feels. Once you are in a relaxed state of mind (and hence, a slight trance), shift your awareness to your skin. Feel the energy pulsating on

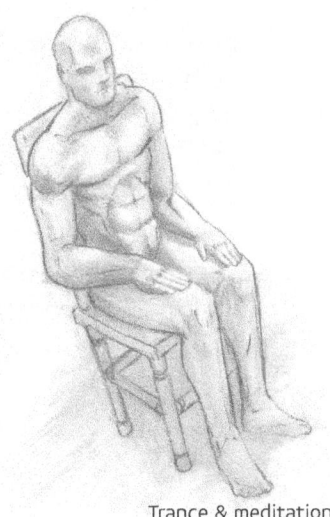

Trance & meditation (sitting) position

and through it, dancing on its surface. Having established the feel of this, refocus on the fact that you are inside your skin. Feel all your outer physical body (Lik) as being a glove, which you are in. It is from this part of you, which is inside, from where this radiating pulse you feel pulsing steadily out of your skin originates. It might take a little while, but keep practising until you get all these sensations in place. Then repeat it for as many times as you need to, in order to be able to switch into that mode of perception in an instant or two at most.

This, ladies and gents, is you sensing the core of the energy body (Hamr) and from it the first and most intense energetic radiation outward. As you progress, keep expanding how far out you can feel the pulse flow. For some, it will not be

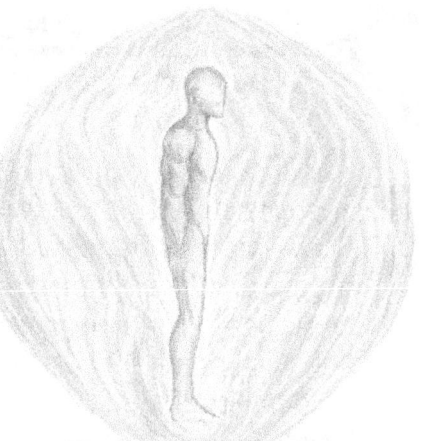

Spherically shaped energy body

too far, while for others, it will be much further out. The average human being has a three-foot radiation, at which point you hit the inner 'skin' or 'shell' of your spherical shape. With a little dedication you should be able to extend this practice to the point where you find yourself walking down the street feeling the energy body (Hamr) core directing the physical movement AND feeling its full spherical/egg shape moving. Eventually, you can perceive yourself as a sphere of energy moving forward when walking down the street.

When doing this, it is important to not only focus on the front of the body – far too much of our awareness is directed forward, so make sure you focus on being able to do this through the back as well and the sides, and above and below. Remember, the energy body (Hamr) is spherical, so you will find it in all directions! Becoming skilled in this is essential before moving onto any other practice. At this stage, you are establishing the foundation of energy body (Hamr) perception which in turn leads you to control.

With a little dedication, you should be able to extend this practice to the point where you find yourself walking down the street, feeling the energy body (Hamr) core directing the physical movement, AND feeling its full spherical shape moving. Eventually, you can perceive yourself as a sphere of energy moving forward when walking down the street with little to no effort.

Egg shaped energy body

Quick Steps

1. Start by sitting in a chair with legs together and arms on the legs (quads). Remain still and breathe, relaxing, allowing all tension to dissipate.
2. Focus on your body, on its physicality and how solid it feels.
3. You should notice the slight pulse of energy on your skin (providing you have remained

perfectly still). Enjoy its dance and motion on and through your skin's surface.

4 Concentrate that YOU, and your very presence and persona, are on the inside of your skin. If it helps, you can imagine it as how a layer of clothing would feel. It is from the YOU inside the skin that this energy pulse originates, pulsing outwards.

5 Repeat these initial steps until you no longer need to put additional effort to trigger the perception(s).

6 As you keep doing this, try to expand how far you can feel this outwards energy pulsing. Typical human beings will have a total pulsating radiation of about three feet. At that point, you will sense the Inside Boundary of your sphere. Remember, your sense of Self is the inner part within your body. The Inner Boundary of your spherical energy body shape is what you can think of as the most distant point of your auric field. This makes perfect sense, if you keep in mind that what mankind calls the aura is in fact the largest part of the energy body itself.

7 Repeat as many times as necessary until this awareness of your entire energy body (Hamr) becomes a reflex you can turn on within an instant or two. It is important to do this sensing in a spherical manner, not just focusing on the front of your body or its left or right. Your energy body (Hamr) is ALL around your physical, in ALL directions (including above and below).

8 When you have mastered this, as you walk in the street, turn on this sensory perception

of the energy body (Hamr) in your daily activities. But remember not to allow it to distract you from the physical environment! There is nothing worse than being focussed on it and getting into harm's way because you are ignoring the things around you in the process. This awareness needs to flow SIMULTANEOUSLY to the physical AND you need to have a perfect distinction between the physical and energetic. It is only this way that you can stretch awareness, rather than just shift it to one or the other.

Once you have reached this stage, also focus on the fact that when you get close to other people, your energy sphere overlaps with theirs (they blend into each other). Or if you are strong enough, you can harden the outer layers of your sphere in order to push other energies away around you. Getting to that point simply requires you to focus in on the outer skin of the energy body (Hamr) and intend it to become more solid, to disallow any other energy in. Any energy which hits against such a hardened outer layer will simply flow around its 'shell'. Naturally, there is no need to push your skills to this point for the practices in this book (but it will definitely do you no harm to do so, if you feel like perfecting them!). Remember what we discussed when talking about having fun with respect to the biological awareness. Time to have fun with this!

SEEING THE ENERGY OF THE ENERGY BODY (HAMR) SPHERE

This one is a fun practice! Sit still as you did when doing the 'Perception of the Energy Body' but this time, make sure you are facing a blank wall. As long as it is not painted with too dark a colour, it will work just fine. Once you have achieved the stillness and can feel the energy radiate on the surface of your skin, look straight ahead but focus on the immediate space in front of you, rather than on the wall itself. If you can manage it, sense your sight coming into the physical eye from the energy body (Hamr)'s eyes (remember, its core is shaped like the physical – hence all the organ shapes are, superimposed on each other). If you retain your focus on seeing from the energy body (Hamr) eyes through the physical (Lik) and look at the space in front of you, intend to see the energy there. You are, in effect, trying to see those parts of the energy body (Hamr) which are typically called the aura (see 'spherically shaped energy body image p.130) from inside the energy body (Hamr).

With a bit of practice, you will at first be able to see tiny sparkle-like particles, very much as an energetic type of dust, erratically floating about in all directions. Then, with a little extra practice, you will be able to notice thin waves of energy flowing through those. More than this one cannot put into words, because it will depend entirely on each individual and how your energy body (Hamr) flows. Even with the two things just mentioned (the sparks and flow), these might not be present or be different. It is important for all these practices to make your own observations. Use these just as a guide for what to look out for, but if what you see does not match, that is fine – it will most probably not match. The important thing is that you are seeing something! Always remember, individual differences are a vital key!

Connecting with The Energy Body (Hamr)

Making that connection with the energy body (Hamr) is of critical importance but is also one of the most difficult things we have to do. The first steps always are, are they not? Connecting with the energy body (Hamr) is a mammoth task, not due to complexity or intricacy of the practices (those are actually mind-numbingly simple), but in terms of achievement. You will need a lot of spare energy to make this connection, and here we are not talking about feeling good and refreshed – the energy involved is the energy of awareness and that is very limited for human beings, especially in today's day and age. Even a slight lack of energy and you will be hard pushed, if at all able, to make this connection. Making it is the first step in maintaining it, and developing the ability to re-establish it at will is even more tricky. So why bother? Because it is only by doing so that we can awaken it, and to do that enables it to become a vehicle for our conscious awareness. Being able to shift our primary seat of consciousness from the physical into the energetic is a vital step for both evolution and survival, after death of the physiology. It is only in our energy bodies (Hamr) that we can gain the ability to express our true selves, beyond the constraints imposed upon such expression of Self by physical limitation.

So how do we gain the required energy reserves? If you have been working through *The Spirit of Húnir Awakens*, you will have learnt to limit the unnecessary waste incurred via behaviours, social norms, language, thought and so forth. Having worked through *The Breath of Oðin Awakens*, you will have learnt how to amplify the amount of Megin stored in the Hamingja and circulate it via DNA into the body (Lik) and then subsequently into the energy body (Hamr). Finally, in this book, you will have learnt how, by observing the sanctity of the body and not injuring it, not losing blood and not exposing it to certain energy wastage activities, how to enhance its physicality and thereby energetic gravity, which all contribute to greater energy reserves. Skipping to the chapters dealing with the Shadow body (Sal), you will learn how to add energy from the 'dark matter' regions to your Being, thereby adding an additional layer for use in awakening the energy body (Hamr). Being persistent with all these practices, they will yield sufficient energy to propel you forward. When you come to using actual High Galdr, you will learn to add those runic currents to your energy sources as well.

For the time being, practice what you have learnt so far and to those practices, add the ones given below. It is impossible to know exactly when you have sufficient energetic resources for this other than by practising it until it all falls into place (otherwise referred to as 'all clicking into place'). This is due to the fact that each individual will have different energy requirements, with some energy body (Hamr) awakening very rapidly with little effort, whilst others seeming to require a climb up Mount Everest! Do not despair if it takes you a long time. The more powerful the energy body (Hamr) and the more scope it has, the more difficult it is to awaken. Once it does, it also takes more energy to maintain and nourish than a quickly awakening one with more limited scope. In any case, as you as you start to see energy, you are on the right track. If you are able to see non-physical beings, you are already awake and just need to nourish it more. Those who as children have developed these skills and have maintained them throughout their lives have fast-awakening energy bodies.

Establishing The Connection

This is a very simple practice. Start off by spending a few minutes relaxing and allowing your mind to clear out all the daily nonsense it is usually preoccupied with. Just think 'relax' and take a few deep breaths to let go of the world around you. You will feel tension flooding out of your body of its own accord. There is no need for any complex tighten-loosen practices – those just cause disturbances in the entire process. Close your eyes and relax. Simple, effective. This will place you in a mild relaxed-trance state. That is all you need here.

The actual step involved is only one. Intend to connect with the energy body (Hamr), harmonise and become one with it. If you like, you can also intend to perceive from WITHIN it. That is all you need to do. Naturally, this requires mastery of intent, but seeing as we have covered that, you should at least have some basic skill in it. All you do here is intend and unleash that intent over and over and over again. Providing the energy is there, you will at first find yourself either in the energy body (Hamr) itself or you will perceive from within it. The first few times, it is only a very short shift, hence a limited experience, but it is profound no matter how long it lasts. The more often you do this and the more energy you build up, the longer it will last and the sharper it will become, until you are building the required 'connections' and with each attempt, you are pushing forward. Eventually, if you persist at it, that proverbial wall will crack and break!

Gender Advantages

Because of our physiological differences and due to the fact that each organ within our body has not only a biological function but also an energetic one, we all have certain strengths (and weaknesses) when it comes to this type of work.

Men have the ability to enhance their intent via the secondary functions of their testicles. Women have an incredibly enhanced perceptive advantage when it comes to energy perception in general, by using the secondary function of their vagina. We will look at these in detail when it comes to dealing with sexual Seiðr practices. For the time being, the best way to make use of these is to 'switch them on' before doing the practice given above.

How you do so is just as inherently simple. Perform the same relaxation as outlined above, then focus on the organ(s) in question (for men, BOTH the testicles and for women, the whole of the vagina). You need to feel them, then simply intend them to increase the power and scope of your intent (for men) or to awaken full perception of the energy level of reality (for women). Go slow with these, as they can cause large changes in your energy system (for both the physical and the energy body (Hamr)).

If you are missing these organs, unfortunately, there is nothing you can do about it and the only course of action is to skip this altogether. Some will argue that even after having the organ removed it is still in the blueprint (the energy body). That is correct, but what is in the blueprint is exactly that: the blueprint for generating the organ, NOT the organ itself. What we are using here is the energetic function of the PHYSICAL organs. The sexual organs and their correct functioning are very important when working with the energy body (Hamr), the shadow body (Sal) and the physical body (Lik). There is simply no escaping that.

If in doubt, skip this practice and do the main one given above. It will take longer but will not stop you from achieving your goal.

This, ladies and gents, should provide you with all the main key pre-requisites needed. The only thing left to cover is Intent and visualisations (discussed below). Remember to work with the energy body (Hamr) and your biological awareness on a regular basis they are both your starting ground (in terms of evolution) AND the two keys to making your runic work manifest in the energy level of reality (which includes the physical!).

INTENT

The Great Mystery of Intent

Intent is a very important concept to grasp and is an extremely important skill to master. It is what fuels action, movement, motion and evolution itself. On the energetic side of reality, all is based around intent. It is the foundation of everything else you will ever do, in one way or another. Without it, nothing happens. Actually, the more you move from the physical into the deeper layers of energetic existence, the closer you will get to the point where nothing can exist without intent. It is a simple principle of 'no intent – no existence' because at those levels, intent is what causes existence. It is, in fact, existence's fundamental cause.

What Exactly Is Intent?

There is no point in discussing the dictionary definition of intent because here we are focussing on the fundamental action of Spirit (Óðr) and not of its tool (the mind). Linguistics is capped at the mind level. We are seeking to move beyond the ceiling of the intellect, which is most difficult to convey in writing. We will try and formulate as much of it as possible, to guide you to the actuality of intent. You will have to use the following information as a map towards the nature and experience of intent, not as a 'this is it' type of indicator. Why so? Intent is felt, or to be more precise, it is sensed and experienced. It is not thought or reasoned. Remember the sense of the Spirit (Óðr)? That is how you know intent as a direct sensory input at the level of your Spirit (Óðr).

Let us hence try to conceptualise intent. Broadly speaking, it can be thought of as an impulse of the Will manifesting from within your own spirit into the outer or inner worlds. In other words, it is a manifestation of the most subtle form of activity of the Spirit (Óðr), the Spark of Self sending out an impulse of what it wills. This gives intent a cohesive energetic manifestation. Intent has energy, direction, flow and purpose. It expresses the Will of the Spirit (Óðr) as well as its nature. Understanding what our Will actually is, is also critical to gaining a solid concept of intent.

Limitations Imposed Upon Intent

At this point in evolution, intent is limited in one key manner. It has been only manifest at the mental level of reality. Without a physical body (Lik), it has been unable to intend at the energetic and physical levels of existence. When discussing the energy level, it is important to keep in mind that what is being described is not that the mental level lacks energy – quite the contrary. It is a total flurry of energetic flows but there is no cohesive energy substance. It is a level of thought which directs energy, rather than a level of energy per se. Only once the cohesion of energy takes place and forms energetic substance, which in turn becomes cohesive in its own right, that we get an energetic level of existence. This is another one of those highly abstract concepts, but it will make sense as you awaken various parts of the Self. They will help you understand these abstractions with such ease that you will at that point wonder what the fuss was all about. Once the Spirit (Óðr) has gained manifestation into a physical form and formed its energetic form, it then becomes capable of expressing intent in its completeness. This is one of the primary reasons why we learn to express intent on the mental level first and then progress onto the energetic. We are in effect following the flow of manifestation and enhancing the totality of possible ways for intent to be expressed.

At that point, intent is still the expression of the Will of Óðr as an impulse streaming from it, but it also gains a distinct energetic quality to it AND gains the expression of conscious awareness. It no longer is one but is now three principles flowing in union. This is true complete intent. As such, in order to learn how to intend, the learning has to be done at both the mental level via the practices of the Spirit (Óðr) and at the physical level via the practices of the energy body (Hamr). Only then can we unleash true intent. It is this form of intent which shapes realities and the Self, which is why, when using High Galdr, understanding and developing one's ability to practically use intent is so vitally important. It is one of its fundamentals which turns Galdr from just repetitive chanting of the runic names into an actual expression of reality-shaping intent (High Galdr). This is why Húnir's gift is so important to us all, as it is the perfect way to express higher forms of consciousness in Midgard.

The methods for mastering intent span across many practices in this work. Let us then move onto the first part of these without further ado.

It is of vital importance to master intent. The full capabilities of it, once all the parts are combined, is a direct manifestation of one's actual Spark of Self. Fuelled by the power of Megin-filled breath (Önd), rooted in the energy body (Hamr) and flowing through the Spirit (Óðr), intent is the root of all power. Ensure you master this and all parts of the intent well. It is an essential key. Work on your intent, strengthen it and empower it each and every day. Unleash it over and over again. Unleash multiple intents simultaneously. Keep pushing forth more and more. Develop and enhance your intent every moment you can. All future work will require intent mastery.

Mastering Intent - Part I
Pure Thought

We have said much with respect to the mind-reason (Hugr) thus far, but little practical groundwork with respect to the Spirit (Óðr) has been presented. It is time for that to change! Communicating with the Spirit (Óðr) is a little tricky, to say the least, but once you get used to it, it becomes the easiest thing you can do. Because the Spirit (Óðr) is the thought processor and generator, you cannot communicate in terms of linguistic thought. As soon as you add words to your thoughts, they are no longer abstract enough to reach the Spirit (Óðr) and instead reach the Hugr-Minni level. This is why so many people struggle with even becoming aware of their Spirit (Óðr). What we need to use in order to communicate is what can be termed pure thought.

The best way to comprehend pure thought is to think of it in terms of meaning or conceptions of what you want to communicate, rather than the words you would use to label it. For instance, if you try to tell it to expand your awareness, you would focus on sensing what the meaning behind expansion of awareness is.

It is extremely difficult to explain but it is a type of sensing what the words are trying to describe. This sense flows either directly to where you are aiming your communication or through the energies you send out and receive. You are basically wrapping thousands of words into a single sense of meaning. This will take time to master but once things click and you understand what you are trying to do, it will become child's play. In order to do this from a practical perspective, all you need to do is to learn how to convey what you would in terms of words but without ever using a word, and then imagine feeling what you are trying to convey. It is a subtle type of sensing of meaning wrapped in non-verbal thought. The best way to try and explain it is simply to try to perceive how you decide to cross a street, or do something physically in the automated way you do, without thinking about it. For instance, when you walk, you are moving, but you do not think about the moving. We have no need to think, 'Ok, I'm going forward for 10 paces, then moving a little to the left or right and then turning around'. Instead, we just intend to do this without forming a single actual set of thoughts using words. We move using intent wrapped in pure thought. The same happens when you pick up a cup and make tea. It is automatic yet also directed, thoughtlessly.

Once you master pure thought, you have in effect mastered the mental part of actual intent. When working with energy, be it runic energy or energy of any other type, intent plays an essential role. Typically, one would attempt to manipulate and direct energy with thought alone; however, herein lies a big problem. How the energy you work with interprets the directing thought(s) will depend on the energy and whether you are able to think abstractly enough to filter out the human thinking patterns and idiosyncrasies. Using intent rather than just thought avoids the entire problem, allowing you to intend the desired result in such an abstract manner that any type of energy will natively understand what you want it to do. This removes the entire problem of things not manifesting, or manifesting in not quite the way you want them to, all of which are results of 'interpretation' of thoughts. Remember, you are in effect communicating with the underlying consciousness – or rather awareness – of that energy.

For instance, if you send out some healing via the ᚢ Úr (Uruz) rune to your partner and think-heal him/her, typically you would visualise that limb (such as a leg) which is injured. The runic energy will be confused as to whether it is healing the physical leg, what part of it, when, how or if it is healing the energetic counterpart of the leg. Or is it both? Does it heal from physical to energetic? Or the other way around? What do you mean by healing? If you try to pack all that information in, you risk even more misinterpretations when using words. Then you have the issue of energy-specific interpretations and adaptations. Healing in terms of ᚢ Úr (Uruz) is regeneration. It would not be very effective in the case of a flu infection. However, if you think 'heal' in context of ᚦ Þurs (Thurisaz), that would work on the flu, as it would attack and strike at the actual virus. If you think 'heal' for regeneration in terms of ᚦ Þurs (Thurisaz), it will cause tissue breakdown and inflammation in order to initiate the body's own repair mechanism, rather than actually heal. As you can see, this subtle difference of adaptation of the term 'heal' causes a lot of problems.

With pure thought, the meaning behind the term 'heal' is used instead, programming each energy automatically. So if you use the pure thought of 'heal' and ᚦ Þurs (Thurisaz), aiming it at the torn muscle, it will not cause tissue breakdown but rather quicken blood flow and increase neural conductivity there, which helps the body rebuild or heal faster. This is a very important difference.

Do not let this complexity bog you down for the time being. Simply work at learning pure thought until you have mastered it.

Mastering Intent - Part II
Biological Sensing

It is now time to look at the second part of intent. We have seen above that intent requires what is called pure thought, or otherwise language, image, sound and sensation-less thought, or pure impulse.

Once that has been mastered, you will be one third of the way to full mastery of intent – well actually, more like half way there. The second part is sensation. In order to unleash intent, you will need bodily sensation to be fused with the pure thought. Combined, these two form actual intent and are the basis for intent-driven consciousness and actions. This is a basis of creation and runic Galdr as well as the key requirement for a lot of Seiðr.

Gaining the sensory element of intent is a bit of a tricky one but not really difficult. The first step involves feeling the entire body. Just relax, still yourself and feel your body, letting your awareness of the sensations of the body flood your thoughts. Having gained a good solid sensing of the physical body (Lik), unleash your pure thought into it and allow it to merge with the body's sensations. For instance, intend to calm the physical systems in your body. Your intent is calm relaxation and peacefulness – or if you prefer, stillness. Once you have that as a pure thought, sense your body.

Having gained a solid sense of your body, allow the pure thought of calmness to flood your entire body and merge with your sense of it. For those who have a keen sense of perception, a change in the type of bodily sensation will take place and be more than noticeable. Allow this new intent sensation to flood every single cell of your body, to merge with it. When your entire physiology is sensing and responding to that intent-fuelled sense (in harmony with it), simply allow your biological awareness to flood you and you will have actual intent. You will see them merge, the sensations of intent arising in your physical body (Lik) and the biological awareness, and this fusion – or rather, the result of it – is actual intent. You should not worry too much about understanding it logically. All that is required are the sensations. This part of intent is purely physiological and sensory.

It may seem a long, tedious process, but the more you practice, the faster and easier it gets. The initial problem is simply that people seldom really intend, they do not know how to, or even that it is possible to do. It is the same situation as a child learning to walk – damn hard work if you ask the child, but an automatic no-challenge act, if you ask the adult. This is exactly the same, because intent is actually unleashed by the body, not the mind. In time, it will be a matter of simply:

1. Getting the pure thought of what is to be intended
2. Allowing the physiological sensation of that

intent to be unleashed as directed by the will.
3. Unleashing your biological awareness and allowing it to flood the mix of pure thought flowing through the respective bodily sensations.

Very fast and simple. You should not worry about it for now. Simply focus on mastering the individual stages. For those of you who are following this closely, you will now realise just why the physical body (Lik) is so critically important in terms of spiritual evolution. Without learning to unleash intent, it would be a great challenge very few could achieve, if not impossible.

- Roadmap to High Galdr Rune Work -

Mastering Intent – Part III
Streaming of Intent

This is more of an application or extension of intent, rather than mastery thereof. Once you have a good grasp of unleashing it as a single event, the next stage is to stream it as a flow. This simply requires you intending to intend as a flow of whatever you are aiming to intend. How is that for a mind loop! Start off with your intent, then get to the point where you have the sensation of all your cells in your body sensing the intent and unleashing it. The result of this is that the intent which is initiated as pure thought in your mind – an impulse of pure thought – is then felt by every cell in your body (in other words, the full extent of your biological awareness). This amplifies and condenses it, and then you unleash it. At that moment, you initiate a second flow of the same intent and bring it to the point where the cells are in harmony with the sensing of that second intent. Simply unleash them both at the same time. Job done! The original intent will flow as a stream of willed intent. Their energy should fuse into a single streaming wave of intending until you willingly turn it off or run out of power. A simple 'enough' or 'stop' thought does the trick. This is called 'Streaming of Intent' or 'Intending'. The two labels can be used interchangeably, although the former gives a slightly better understanding of the process for the logical mind.

Quick Steps

1. Start as usual with your intent. Ensure every cell in your body feels it and is echoing the intent (in effect, your biological awareness is intending, alongside your conscious mind). Then unleash it.
2. As you unleash intent, make sure you also intend that unleashed intent to flow (think of it as streaming the intent, if that helps).
3. Then start the process once more through points 1 and 2, and when the cells of your body are vibrating with this second wave, release it alongside the first. Their energy should fuse into a single streaming wave of intending until you willingly turn it off or run out of power. A simple 'enough' or 'stop' thought does the trick.

As usual, practice makes perfect. A master of intending can unleash waves upon waves of intending in such a rapid stream of pure willed awareness that even trying to time it in a matter of one second would be infinitely too slow. Naturally, for the runic work at hand, there is simply no need for that level of intending proficiency. Simply unleashing a single intent will do the trick nicely –, if possible, mastering the streaming of that one intent would be very helpful as well, but beyond that, we are looking at applications which are simply far too advanced for the matter at hand.

Pulling The Self into The Lik

This is where our approach in Norse mysticism differs significantly from practically all other traditions. We bring the higher parts of the Self INTO the physical, rather than seek to escape the physical by merging with the higher. In other words, those parts of the Self become part of our physical and conscious domain. The physical body (Lik) becomes the centre point for all the rest.

The next stage of the practice involves going a step further and bringing into the physical (Lik) all the embodiments of the Self. This includes all other personas we build over the course of our lives, all the perceptions of Self we have: us the parent, us the child, us the husbands, us the wives, us the professional, us the 'whatever your job may be', us the embodiments in our dreams and so forth). All these temporary glimpses of self-embodiment are brought into the physical body (Lik) and merged into biological and conscious awareness.

Some will wonder why on earth use this approach, rather than just seeking to merge out of the physical into the so-called 'higher' parts of the Self. This is for two reasons: one is that the so-called 'higher' parts of the Self are not necessarily higher at all, we only label them as such because they are perceived as being more 'mysterious' and hence more 'exalted' than our normal consciousness. The other is that our personality – and hence, the main expression of our individuality at this point in time – is rooted in the physical body (Lik). We know that when we die, this will dissipate and our Self partly fades and partly returns to the essence type of expression, and remerges with either the ancestral, or other manifestations in creation (such as a descendant for the Hugr, if gifted). This means that you will essentially no longer have a 'complete' Self as you do at this point in time. Hence the teachings on Midgard being the centre of creation, and us children of Midgard being centres of the Self provide us with a very unique opportunity to complete our Selves.

Since the main part of the Self which is responsible for the conscious awareness we have – and hence our personality – is the physical body (Lik), that is our main focus. We bring all that which we can into the physical (Lik) and into the reach of our conscious awareness, rather than losing ourselves by merging into so-called 'higher' forms of expression, which in turn, will have to embody again in a new Self and repeat the cycle until completion (which does include the physical – you cannot complete a whole if you persistently reject one of its parts) is achieved. Some will argue that this is re-incarnation, but it is not. Reincarnation is a concept where 'you' are reborn again to live life anew. But if parts of 'you' are actually dissolved and lost, or flow into another, it is no longer the 'you' that you are. It will be some other form of you, with a new form of consciousness, a new personality and a new expression of the individuality. It is exactly like changing a molecule in a chemical – even the slightest alteration produces a completely new and hence different molecule. This new 'you' is no longer the same, and is no longer 'you'. This new personality is, technically speaking, someone else with your intellect and experiences and abilities as a starting point for which it builds its own Self. 'Yours' is dissipated and some of its parts have been reused.

This, ladies and gents, completes our initial foundational work with the physical body (Lik) and puts us in great standing to being our energy body (Hamr) work. Needless to say, what you have worked through in these few chapters is the tip of the iceberg, but is an essential start. More exciting things to discover? Always. We never end our learning and just as we think we have a solid knowledge and grasp of things, we realise that we have only just breached the threshold. Fun, is it not?

This will provide you will a good solid understanding and skill set when it comes to unleashing runic energy directed by intent. Remember, using intent is how you tell whatever energies, powers, parts of the Self and so forth what you what them to do and how far and wide their effects will be. Do keep in mind that you will need to match the energies or powers with the appropriate intent. It is absolutely foolish to use a frost-based rune to try and heat or speed something up! For the time being, practice your intending. We will cover each of the rune's powers, energies and scope of activity in the next book: *High Galdr: Rune Science - The Ultimate Book of Runes.*

Roadmap to High Galdr Rune Work

VISUALISATION

Roadmap to High Galdr Rune Work

The Art of Visualisation

Everything we do in Norse Mysticism is calculated to produce specific results, so the term 'art' should be avoided when referring to it. This rule can be a little more relaxed, however, when it comes down to visualisations. There are certain tricks to it but ultimately speaking, visualisation is more of a learnt art than a calculated scientific process with a specific result.

Most will wonder why to even enter into discussions relating to visualisation in the first place. Surely everyone can visualise? Well, yes and no. Some people completely lack the ability to form mental imagery, but that is mostly due to an extremely rare brain defect, affecting a handful of individuals globally. Everyone else does have the ability to form mental imagery. Visualisation, however, is not limited to mental imagery. It should include all the senses as well as 'sensing' itself. Hence even if you are one of those rare people who cannot visualise by using mental imagery, you can do so using your other senses.

Forming visualisations brings all senses together, so whatever you are visualising must include seeing (imagery), hearing (sound), sensations (feeling), smelling (odour) and, if possible, tasting. To these, we are going to add sensing. Most think that because the term visualisation is composed of 'visual' and '-isation', it out of necessity requires only the visual imagery components or visual processes. This is why so many visualisations actually fail to produce any actual results. One sense alone does not have sufficient empowering effects to solidify whatever it is you are visualising. The senses of taste and smell can be very tricky, but remember that young children explore the world (initially) by putting everything in their mouths, thereby touching and tasting things. You need to do the same whenever possible. Involve ALL your senses.

Once all five senses are involved, you will need to add sensing itself, which as we discussed before, is the sense of the spirit (Óðr). Unless you can spiritually 'read' or 'sense' whatever it is you are visualising, then it simply does not exist.

One important thing to keep in mind is that the primary five senses are a manifestation of touch. When you see, what is actually happening is your eyes are touching the light that objects and people reflect. (If they absorbed it, you would see them as a black object.) As the light touches your eyes' corona, it triggers electrical impulses in the brain which are interpreted as upside down images. The brain inverts them for you, which incidentally confuses those who start to project out of their bodies to no end since the brain no longer does this for them. A similar thing occurs with all the other senses. Hearing occurs when sound waves touch your inner ears (incidentally you can also feel sound waves), feeling when your skin makes contact with something or someone, smell when odour touches receptors in the nasal passages and tasting involves a multitude of touch-based inputs, as outlined below:

> "But what is taste actually? What happens in our body that enables us to perceive flavor? The chemical substance responsible for the taste is freed in the mouth and comes into contact with a nerve cell. It activates the cell by changing specific proteins in the wall of the sensory cell. This change causes the sensory cell to transmit messenger substances, which in turn activate further nerve cells. These nerve cells then pass information for a particular perception of flavor on to the brain [...]
>
> What is generally categorized as "taste" is basically a bundle of different sensations: it is not only the qualities of taste perceived by the tongue, but also the smell, texture and temperature of a meal that are important. The "coloring" of a taste happens through the nose. Only after taste is combined with smell is a food's flavor produced. If the sense of smell is impaired, by a stuffy nose for instance, perception of taste is usually dulled as well."[5]

In other words, the sense of taste is a product of multiple manifestations of touch. Pure sensing works on this basis, too. When your Spirit (Óðr) touches energy, mental formations of concepts and abstractions and so forth. Ultimately, it is all one single sense manifesting in a number of different ways.

Now you can understand why involving all the senses will strengthen your visualisations. Instead of a single touch, that visualisation will be experiencing **six** of them at a time. Doing all of this in your visualisation technique will add energy to it and we have seen how energy plus thought leads to manifestation. Interestingly, the sixth rune in the first Ætt is ᚲ Kaun (Kenaz), which points to the concept of controlled (under will) fire (empowerment). Here we introduce a bit of runic numerology for you to consider!

Mastering visualisation requires one final step, and that is imbuing it with intent. Everything in Creation has purpose, directionality and energy. We have looked at how to imbue these visualisations with as much energy as possible, and how the last stage of pushing that thought and energy combination into manifestation involved imbuing it with actual intent. Intent will give it purpose and, with the addition of purpose, it gains directionality.

Typically, with runic energy work, we automatically imbue our visualisations with some intent. After all, there is a reason we are doing the visualising in the first place. Actual intent, however, will amplify this to unmeasurable levels. You have learnt the basics regarding the mystery of intent above. Use those skills or practice to imbue your visualisations with more intent. Mastering this is critically important because it will enable you to make rapid progress in your energy manipulation and usage abilities.

Positioning Visualisations

Most will wonder what on earth is meant by positioning visualisations. It becomes relevant only whilst visualising when in your physical body (Lik), energy body (Hamr) and/or shadow (Sal). So what is this positioning all about? In short, it has to do with how visualisations interact and are interpreted whilst you are in one of your bodies on the energetic level of reality (or the Self, for that matter). Let us put this right into context, in order to avoid causing any confusion. When in your physical body on a daily basis, you see straight ahead of you and, to a limited extent, to the periphery of

- Visualisation -

yourself (called the peripheral vision range). The eyes are receptive organs of the brain. Note the word 'receptive', which means they are receivers first and foremost. What happens when most people visualise? Typically, you form your images in front of you, out of sensory habit learned from sight. What this causes is you trying to see again – you are 'projecting' something by using a receiving mechanism. See the problem? It is like turning a power switch off and wondering why your computer is not on and working. The current is in the wrong position (off rather than on). The same happens when you try to project your field of vision to the front of you and its peripheral range. Anything you visualise, no matter how fantastic your visualisation skills are or how much detail you have put into it, no matter how powerful the intent imbued within it, if projected into your field of vision, it will short-circuit and fail because this is how you receive environmental information on both the physical and the energetic. On the mental level of reality, there is no such thing as directionality, and therefore, it cannot short circuit. As soon as you force it to manifest on the energetic, however, directionality and shape come into play. By positioning the visualisation on the receptive area, you are wasting all your hard work, time and energy. This is a big no-no!

    The trick is to visualise – or rather, project – your visualisation OUTSIDE of the range of vision, or just on the border, so that it is mostly outside but can have a little part crossing over into the field of vision. This applies to open eye visualisation AND closed eye visualisation. When you are doing it with eyes shut and staring at the black background of your closed eyelids, ALWAYS make sure you are visualising outside of your field of vision, because the eyes (and especially, later on, the energy body (Hamr) eyes) are still receiving information there. The only issue being that they are receiving blackness of the back of your eyelids – but receiving nonetheless they are!

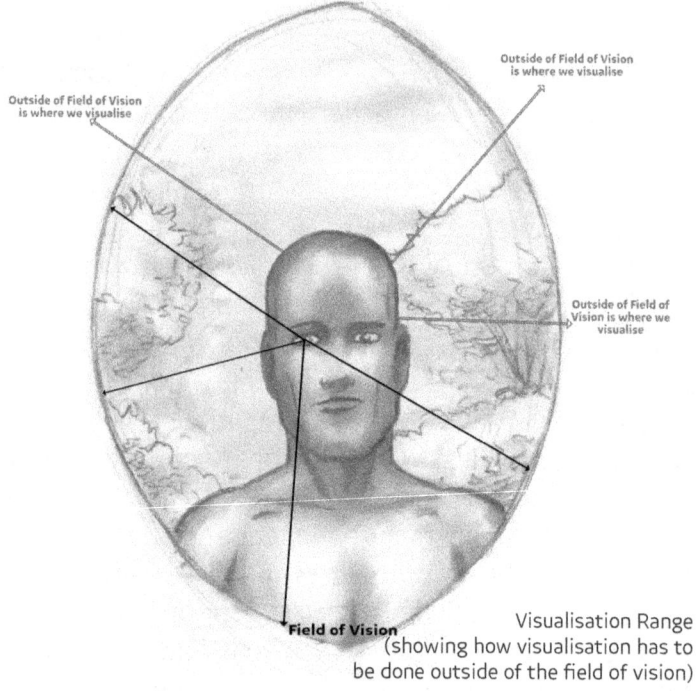

Visualisation Range
(showing how visualisation has to be done outside of the field of vision)

As soon as you start visualising OUTSIDE of your field of vision, you are pushing your visualisations into energetic reality and, in time (depending on the amount of energy and strength of intent), into the densest parts thereof (in other words, the physical). This, ladies and gents, is the key to visualising! And the key to not failing. It is also the reason why, except in projections of Self, you always focus on being in vast empty space all around you, and you visualise the runic energies all around you. Yes, some parts will hit the visual range, but most will not!

Visualisation Vs Imagination

This is a topic of immense confusion because a lack of understanding is usually present when comparing these two activities of the mind. There is imagination and imagination. Even more confused? Not to worry. There are different types of imagination. We most often encounter the first type when we try to recall something and imagine it instead. In other words, we imagine what we want to remember, instead of the actual events as they happened. We have seen in *The Spirit of Húnir Awakens (Part 1) p.32* how the brain fails to distinguish between a memory and an imaginary occurrence. The other form of imagination surfaces when we are wishing for something or desiring something, most often during daydreaming and those endless 'what ifs' people have a habit of engaging in. Another manifestation of this type of imagination happens when we are driven by emotion. In this case, we imagine scenarios such as the perfect romantic outing or partner, how we will get revenge or how we will accomplish a much-desired goal. The final type of imagination we encounter happens when visualising, which we will call 'directed, willed imagination'. Why is this different? Because it has purpose, function and focus which the other types do not have – they have wishful thinking or impulse reaction instead, but no 'dimensionality'.

When visualising, we are taking imagination and making it an active tool of the mind, controlled and directed by our will. This gives it a dimensionality which other forms of imagination do not naturally have. In this way, it is something more than just imagination. Because the modern mind loves to dabble in the 'but is it real' nonsense, let us look into that right now and put the whole issue into our 'resolved' box.

So, is this type of imagination real? Yes. Not as real as a physical object by any stretch, but it is real nonetheless. Once you use willed and directed imagination, you are gathering into it all the hallmarks of the things needed to manifest your desire from the mental into the energetic levels. As more and more energy, intent and, most importantly, thought coalesces into whatever it is we have wilfully imagined, it echoes out on the mental level and pulls more of what is like it into itself, propelling it faster and faster into a more tangible reality. In effect, you are using imagination, under willed direction, to bridge things into reality. Your energy body (Hamr) and even your physical body (Lik) will eventually start reacting to it in exactly the same way as it does with actual reality.

This is one of the most fascinating creative powers of our minds – once unlocked, wonders await! So stop wasting your imagination. Seize it by your will and direct it for your own evolution and benefit. Do not waste such an important ability.

Runically speaking, we see the ᚲ Kaun (Kenaz) rune once again in action here. The inspiration of ᚠ Óss

(Ansuz) is directed by the willed imagination (ᚱ Reið (Raidho)) into realisation (ᚲ Kaun (Kenaz)). By crossing the imagined-real point via exchange of energy and intent (ᚷ Gjöf (Gebo)) and harmonised (hence manifests) into actual reality (ᚹ Vin (Wunjo)), it thereafter becomes a part of it. We will look at these runic flows in a lot of detail. Using this rune combination, activating them one after the other can provide you with assistance in speeding up such manifestations into actual reality.

This completes all your foundation skills and will have provided you with not only a dipping of your toes into the mysteries of the Self, but also expanded your base perceptions, awareness and even consciousness to the point where you are now in possession of the basic skill sets you need for High Galdr.

It has been a pleasure to guide you to this point and will be an even greater one in the next title, when we finally, at long last, talk RUNES! And not only dispel a lot of the nonsense out there but also look at much deeper levels than practically any other book ever has. Ladies and gents, our next step: **High Galdr: Rune Science - The Ultimate Book of Runes**, where you will learn how to unleash the powers and characteristics of the runes via Galdr, as the Masters and Mystics of Old did.

Frank A. Rúnaldrar

APPENDIXES

APPENDIX A

Table of Runic Names in Icelandic & Germanic

Rune	Numeric Value	Icelandic Name	Germanic Name
ᚠ	1	Fé	Fehu
ᚢ	2	Úr	Uruz
ᚦ	3	Þurs	Thurisaz
ᚨ	4	Óss (Ás)	Ansuz
ᚱ	5	Reið	Raidho
ᚲ	6	Kaun	Kenaz
ᚷ	7	Gjöf	Gebo
ᚹ	8	Vin	Wunjo
ᚺ	9	Hagall	Hagalaz
ᚾ	10	Nauð	Nauthiz
ᛁ	11	Íss	Isa
ᛃ	12	Ár	Jera
ᛈ	13	Perð	Pertho
ᛇ	14	Jór	Eihwaz
ᛉ	15	Ýr	Elhaz
ᛋ	16	Sól	Sowilo
ᛏ	17	Týr	Tiwaz
ᛒ	18	Bjarkan	Berkano
ᛖ	19	Eykur	Ehwaz
ᛗ	20	Maður	Mannaz
ᛚ	21	Lögur	Laguz
ᛜ	22	Ing	Ingwaz
ᛞ	23	Dagur	Dagaz
ᛟ	24	Óðal	Othala

Roadmap to High Galdr Rune Work

APPENDIX B

References & footnotes

1. Strange Footprints on the Land (Author: Irwin, Constance publisher: Harper & Row, 1980) ISBN 0-06-022772-9)

2. Snorri Sturluson. The Prose Edda: Tales from Norse Mythology, translated by Jean I. Young (University of California Press, 1964)

3. Simon J. Greenhill; Ross Clark; Bruce Biggs (2010). 'Protoform: MANA.1 [OC] Power, effectiveness, prestige'. Polynesian Lexicon Project Online.

4. Marett, R. R. (1914) [1909]. The Threshold of Religion (Second, Revised and Enlarged ed.) London: Methuen and Co. Ltd. p.12-13

5. Institute for Quality and Efficiency in Health Care (2016), "How does our sense of taste work?", Informed Health Online, retrieved from: http://www.ncbi.nlm.nih.gov/pubmedhealth/PMH0072592/

- Roadmap to High Galdr Rune Work -

FORTHCOMING TITLES

High Galdr: Rune Science
The Ultimate Book of Runes

Runes, runes and more runes! The sacred science of the Gods, the runes were made available to their children, our Ancestors. Much information is available about the runes, yet so very little is known as to how they are actually used. They are chanted, they are written, and they are drawn. Yet all these methods fail to produce rapid or tangible manifestations.

Using the runes is a science and, like any science, the rules under which its principles operate need to be known. Unleashing a runic vocalisation using proper Galdr has been kept secret for ages, known to only an extremely select few who were capable of mastering their very Self. These methods for Galdr were passed down through generations as part of our vocal tradition, with only sparse written instruction preserved.

At long last, actual methods and underlying principles of manifesting the power of the runes are being made available unabridged with no hidden facets, no secret methods left unturned. Learn at long last how to wield the runes, how to unleash and manifest them, how to recode reality and reform events in life using the heritage left to us by our Ancestors and living with-in our DNA. Each and every rune holds a secret, a key, a power, a source of knowledge and a potential.

Learn to unleash it ALL with actual High Galdr.

DreamWalking
The Art of Runic Dreaming

Dreaming, everyone does it, yet not everyone remembers it, some like it others fear it but no one can agree on what dreaming actually is and why we all dream. Science argues it is a result of the brain consolidating daily information and memories, Psychology argues it is a reflection of the inner state of being and mental balance, mystics argue it is a separation of the spirit from the body and so forth.

In Runic dreaming we explore and learn how to both use dreams and grow through them. Combining High Galdr with the Arts of the Völva (Old Norse Prophetess or Seeress) the full power of dreaming is unleashed as a transformation or awakening tool, an essential in reclaiming the full power of human awareness as it takes its first steps across creation.

Learn about runic energy and its impact on dreams, how to remember your dreams and use memory as a gauge of development, how to imbue the Minni (memory) to enhance dream capabilities, how to increase energy via dreams, how to experience the other Nine Worlds through dreams and how to bridge the dream and daily realities to shape the one through the other and vice versa...

Roadmap to High Galdr Rune Work

www.ingramcontent.com/pod-product-compliance
Lightning Source LLC
Chambersburg PA
CBHW031312150426
43191CB00005B/194